LEARN NLP

MASTER NEURO-LINGUISTIC PROGRAMMING (THE NON-BORING WAY) IN 30 DAYS

TONY WRIGHTON

LEGAL BIT

Serious, but necessary. The information in this book has been provided for informational, educational and entertainment purposes only. It is not designed to replace or take the place of any form of therapy or professional medical advice. The information contained in this book has been compiled from sources deemed reliable, and it is accurate to the best of the Author's knowledge; however, the Author cannot guarantee its accuracy and validity and cannot be held liable for any errors or omissions. Upon using the information contained in this book, you agree to hold harmless the Author, and Publisher, from and against any damages, costs, and expenses, including any legal fees potentially resulting from the application of any of the information provided by this guide. This disclaimer applies to any damages or injury caused by the use and application, whether directly or indirectly, of any advice or information presented, whether for breach of contract, tort, negligence, personal injury, criminal intent, or under any other cause of action. You agree to accept all risks of using the information presented inside this book. Legal bit over. Now, let's learn NLP (the non-boring way). Copyright © 2022 Tony Wrighton

ABOUT THE AUTHOR

Tony Wrighton is a UK-based journalist and broadcaster. His books have been translated into 12 languages, including Spanish, Italian, Japanese, Chinese, Turkish, Dutch and Croatian.

His broadcasting career has spanned two decades, being a regular presenter on channels including Sky News, Sky Sports News, ITV and LBC. He also hosts a podcast called *Zestology*.

He started training in Neuro-Linguistic Programming (NLP) in 2004. Over the years, he has progressed to the top of the field in these skills (Practitioner, Master Practitioner and Trainer). He is also qualified in Emotional Freedom Therapy (EFT) and a registered Mind Factor coach, and loves combining these skills with his background as a journalist.

OTHER 30 DAY TITLES

Stop Scrolling: 30 Days to Healthy Screen Time Habits (Without Throwing Your Phone Away)

CONTENTS

Introduction 13

Day 1 – Get Into Vegas Mode 21
    Anchoring

Day 2 – Get A Connection (But Don't Get The Sack) 25
    Mirroring

Day 3 – What Would You Love, Love, Love To Achieve? 29
    Goals, Outcomes and HUGGs

Day 4 – Communicate (A Bit) Better 34
    Senses (Representational Systems)

Day 5 – Improve Your Memory, Eyesight & Brainpower 39
    Association and Dissociation

Day 6 – In Praise Of Variety 44
    The Law Of Requisite Variety

Day 7 – Don't Trust The GPS 48
    The Map Is Not The Territory

Day 8 – Counting Chimneys 52
    Eye Accessing Cues

Day 9 – Change Your Perspective 56
    Reframes

Day 10 – How To Learn To Play Bach's Concerto In D 60
    Modeling

Day 11 – Throw Out The Alarm Clock 64
   The Unconscious Mind

Day 12 – Chunking Up and Chunking Down 68
   Chunking

Day 13 – Subliminal Messages – Do They Work? 72
   Affirmations

Day 14 – Please Don't Read This 76
   NLP And Language

Day 15 – Make Outrageous Ideas Succeed 79
   The Disney Strategy

Day 16 – Construct A Mind Pyramid 82
   Logical Levels

Day 17 – High Levels Of Focus And Deep Relaxation 87
   Hypnosis

Day 18 – Hypnotic Language Patterns 91
   The Milton Model

Day 19 – Unwanted Thoughts Suck 96
   The Swish Technique

Day 20 – Dealing With Phobias 99
   Fast-Phobia Cure

Day 21 – NLP And Your Notifications 103
   The Pattern Interrupt

Day 22 – Decision-Making 107
   Congruence
   Logical Levels

Day 23 – Let Me Tell You A Story 111
    Storytelling
    Rich, Sensory Language

Day 24 – Mood Boosters 115
    Chaining Anchors
    Tech Anchoring

Day 25 – Improve Your Relationships 119
    Perceptual Positions

Day 26 – Winning At Life 122
    Affirmations
    Dissociation
    Anchoring
    Non-Verbal Communication
    SWISH! Technique

Day 27 – Anxiety Is Horrible 126
    Dissociation
    Instant State Change

Day 28 – Are You Crazy Enough To Believe You Can Change The World? 130
    Limiting Beliefs

Day 29 – The Zeigarnik Effect 133
    Nested Loops
    NLP and Motivation

Day 30 – And The Winner Is… 137
    Is This The Most Useful NLP Technique?

Take another *30 Day Expert* program 140

References 145

WHAT TO EXPECT

In this *30 Day Expert* program, you will quickly and effectively learn Neuro-Linguistic Programming (the non-boring way).

Warning: This is not a dry NLP textbook. Expect stories, examples, interactive real-life scenarios and behavioral science studies throughout.

Each day is a mini-chapter containing an NLP technique you can learn and use straightaway. Here's what you might want to use the skills for:

- Feel happier or more confident
- Achieve your goals
- Improve your relationships
- Inspire others
- Get creative
- Improve/"hack" your presentation skills
- Feel more motivated
- Be more persuasive
- Improve at sport
- Get over a phobia
- And lots, lots more

NLP is an effective and proven set of tools, but it can sometimes seem confusing. Not here though. This program is designed to be easy to complete in 30 days. So let's get started…

INTRODUCTION

Here is one question I get asked a lot.

Er, what exactly is NLP?

Neuro-Linguistic Programming (NLP) helps us improve the way we communicate with ourselves and other people. It studies "what works". It is a wildly popular set of skills and theories first developed in the 1970s; perhaps "neuro-hacking" would be a better name. Here's why it's worth studying it in this *30 Day Expert* program.

- NLP is brilliant for your personal development and the development of others.
- NLP improves your communication.
- NLP helps you manage your moods (this is a biggie).
- NLP helps you get stuff done.
- NLP is used a lot in business, self-improvement, sport, sales, therapy and coaching.

"We were born with a brain, but nowhere are we given instructions for our brain. That is what NLP gives you!"

– Rubin Alaie

My experience of learning NLP has always been that the skills themselves are epic, but sometimes the way it is taught is a little complicated. So my goal in this, and indeed all the *30 Day Expert* books, is to make the subject as simple and enjoyable to learn as possible. That means teaching it in a different, non-traditional way. I introduce behavioral science and studies throughout and take a sometimes non-linear route through the subject.

Finally, I try to make it as enjoyable and interactive as I can – you will of course be the judge of that.

Wow. So NLP actually works?

It does, and in many different, sometimes surprising ways. When I first started learning NLP many years ago, I was working as a radio presenter in Manchester, UK. My teacher impressed on me the importance of practicing these skills as much as possible "in the real world" to get feedback and to improve. He said what was important was to be proficient at using NLP, not just having a piece of paper proclaiming that I was a practitioner.

Good point. A certificate looks nice, but isn't very helpful out in the world. So I came up with a plan. I would practice on the radio. I'd use the linguistic part of NLP to try to make my show better. Ambitious, to say the least. In addition, every radio show wants more listeners. So I would try to encourage new people to listen and to do so for longer too.

For months I used my show as a training ground. It's important to emphasize that I didn't always get it right. In truth, I wasn't very good at this NLP malarkey, but there I was engaging with it and trying to pick it up day after day.

There was one particular afternoon when I felt that I'd been particularly unsubtle. I had been trying out a new skill that I had learned on my course. And, um, it hadn't quite gone to plan. Obviously the only way to improve is to make mistakes and learn from them, but I think on that particular day I just sounded a bit weird.

After I came off air, my boss called me into his office. He sat back and put his hands behind his head. I gulped. I was desperately trying to remember my NLP body language. Were hands behind the head a good thing or not?

"I don't know what you've done," he said, "but your listening figures have gone through the roof."

At that station, I presented the *DriveTime* show. In fact, my listening figures had gone up so much that they had overtaken the *Breakfast Show*. That is something rare in the world of radio.

Was this because of the NLP techniques? Possibly or possibly not. *The Breakfast Show* presenter was brilliant and it may have been luck, advertising or shifting listening habits. But I like to think Neuro-Linguistic Programming had something to do with it.

The reason for telling this story is not a humble brag (okay, maybe a tiny bit). But my NLP teacher told me to "practice, practice practice" and that is what I did. Not only did it help me actually learn, it turned out that the skills worked rather well.

"Everything is practice"

– Pele

Practice is the key thing over the next 30 days. As you read this book, I will encourage you to practice your new NLP skills as much as possible and to embrace the hands-on approach that helped me.

Here are some of the ways NLP is used out in the world.

- People use NLP to achieve their goals, motivate themselves and communicate better. It's especially helpful in relationships.
- Therapists use NLP to help people get over all sorts of life issues, phobias, fears and traumas.
- Top sports stars use NLP to win more. Indeed many of the world's top Performance Coaches are principally trained in NLP.

- Businesses use NLP to help improve their business and inspire their workforce. This is a really big area.
- Salespeople use NLP to sell more. This works scarily well, and always should be done ethically (more on this later)

But what if I want to train traditionally?

Traditional NLP training looks a bit different from this *30 Day Expert* program, but, of course, that would be a great decision too. Old school NLP training levels go like this.

1. **NLP Practitioner.** The first level of qualification. My NLP Practitioner training took five months, but these days you can get a Practitioner certificate in a shorter amount of time. Costs for this training tend to start at around $1,000.
2. **NLP Master Practitioner.** Next-level skills, which helps you to become more elegant and intuitive in your NLP. Often this training costs upwards of $2,000.
3. **NLP Trainer.** Tends to focus on platform and communication skills to deliver an effective message to others. The investment is considerable, and I paid well over $3,000. When you finish NLP Trainer Training, you are qualified to train others in the skills of NLP.

You will of course learn many of the core practitioner skills from this book over the next 30 days, and save yourself some $$$ in the process. It's not exhaustive though. I'm focused on getting you using the best NLP skills with elegance and expertise out in the world. After you've been bitten by the bug I thoroughly recommend you go and explore it further with many of the fantastic NLP schools and teachers out there.

The weird and wonderful language of NLP

NLP specializes in brilliant skills with, admittedly, slightly convoluted names. Here are some of them. (Rest assured I'll demystify them and make them easy to learn):

- Calibration
- Chaining Anchors
- Collapsing Anchors
- Confidence Building Tools
- Complex Equivalence
- Congruence
- Double Bind
- Embedded Commands
- Fast Phobia Cure
- Lack of Referential Index
- Language Patterns
- Logical Levels
- Lost Performative
- Meta Model
- Milton Model
- Mirroring
- Outcomes
- Perceptual Positions
- Presuppositions
- Rapport-building
- Reframing (I love this)
- Swish Pattern
- Timelines

There's some serious jargon in there. But the techniques are simple and brilliant. So to make things easier, in this book we cut through the jargon for something more straightforward. For example, whole chapters could be written on concepts like Complex Equivalence, but I present less complex equivalents. (Apologies for a crap NLP joke there.)

NLP was created in California in the early 1970s by John Grinder and Richard Bandler. The elaborate naming of simple, brilliant techniques was just what they did. I have personally trained with Bandler on a number of occasions and it was memorable.

> **NEURO-LINGUISTIC WHAT?**
>
> As crazy as it sounds, there are many slightly different ways of writing NLP, including Neuro-linguistic Programming, Neuro linguistic programming, and Neuro Linguistic Programming. But this is, after all, a book about NLP, so I had to make a decision.
>
> For the sake of ease, I've used Neuro-Linguistic Programming throughout. It seems to make the most sense and be the most widely used today, though of course it all does the same thing, regardless of the capitalization and hyphenation used.

So can NLP basically save the world?

Uh, no. I have never regarded Neuro-Linguistic Programming as a catch-all set of skills that will solve all the world's problems. It is a very powerful set of skills, and I consider myself very lucky to have progressed to such a high level in NLP. However I have trained in and learned lots of different modalities and I think they all have a place.

For example, from my personal perspective, there are aspects of my life that I could only resolve through deep psychotherapy, and I'm grateful I was able to experience that. NLP has given me many things but, to put it bluntly, it couldn't have solved some of my deep issues.

Do not use these techniques on anyone suffering from psychosis, severe anxiety or suicidal thoughts. For deep trauma, it is not appropriate to use NLP unless highly skilled. You mustn't use these tools on anyone who needs medical help. If in doubt, do not use these techniques and refer to a doctor or professional. This book does not confer a qualification.

I also want to acknowledge that not everybody agrees that NLP is a worthwhile set of skills. That's fine. In the spirit of "doing what works," I believe there are lots of different methods and systems that can work in helping people to change and improve themselves. Science and research are particularly important. I am a pragmatist about what we can achieve with NLP – which is a lot (I believe), but not everything. It's great to keep an open mind.

So yes, learn NLP in 30 days. And then next month, learn something different. It'll only make you an even better communicator.

Using Your Powers For Good

Finally, this may seem a slightly trite superhero saying, but it's important to use your powers for good.

I have been to many NLP-related conferences and seminars around the world. I have met some incredibly talented people who understand Neuro Linguistic Programming inside out. The best of them are genuine, and they interact with authenticity and curiosity. In NLP we might call this *congruence*.

Occasionally, though, I meet somebody who seems a little 'off'.

They might shake my hand rather oddly, so my palm is facing upwards. Or they may use clunky phrases like "you, like me, are interested in learning NLP", thinking they are subtly using an NLP technique known as an embedded command ("you like me!). They seem more interested in how they can bend my way of thinking than in actually being a force for good in the world.

People like this are a rarity but they are rather sad examples of those who aren't acting with total congruence and integrity. (Also, they're normally not very good at NLP anyway.)

> *"Don't fake anything. It's exhausting and unnecessary."*
>
> *– Joanna Penn*

Over the next 30 days, be authentic and be genuine. NLP is not about secretly influencing people, but about creating some good in the world.

> *"Be nice or leave"*
>
> *– Seen on a mug, London*

DAY 1

Get Into Vegas Mode

"I shouldn't be near Vegas and have money in my pocket."
– Adam Sandler

Yep, this quote is probably true for almost all of us. Losing money is no fun. Gambling often ends badly. But what if we were playing with the bank's money in Vegas, rather than our own? Hang on a sec. Now we wouldn't be betting our own hard-earned cash, but somebody else's. This could be fun, as we just couldn't lose.

How would this make you feel?

- Playful?
- Curious?
- Carefree?

These are the sort of ways we want to feel on Day 1 as we learn anchoring.

(Don't worry if you're not a fan of Vegas. You'll soon see that you can tailor this technique to your own happy place.)

Here's how we do it. Scientists have long known the power of "Pavlovian responses", which were named after the famous Russian scientist Ivan Pavlov (1). He would ring a bell as his dogs were being fed. After a while, he could ring the bell, and his dogs would salivate even when there was no food. A stimulus (in this case, food, and then the bell summoning the thought of food) could elicit an automatic response.

This stimulus works by making use of the way the brain links a sensory experience to a thought. Have you ever heard a song, and it's reminded you of a wonderful holiday or a particular time of your life? That's the thing we're talking about. In NLP, it's called anchoring.

It is a core NLP skill, and it comes on Day 1 because you can use it almost anywhere. It's a great place to start.

> *"Anchoring in neuro-linguistic programming sure feels like grand-wizardry, but it's none other than good ole' fashioned neuroscience"*
>
> – Mike Mandel

Vegas Mode

So let's play with anchoring now. We're going to imagine playing with the bank's money in Vegas. Since our brains don't differentiate between real experience and imagined experience, this should be fun...

- You're on a roll.
- You feel like you can do anything.
- You're relaxed about the outcome.
- You're firmly in the present.
- You feel awesome.

You've probably had this feeling in the past. It might have been from doing well at work, winning at sport, or making confident decisions.. Every once in a while, we feel we just can't lose. And it's an incredible feeling.

(Disclaimer. Don't go spend your life savings in Vegas after reading this. I guess it's probably worth pointing out that we're aiming for the feeling of playing with the bank's money, not actually gambling with our own money.)

Anchoring

For this particular version of anchoring, you need a coin – any coin will do. If you've got a roulette chip, so much the better.

1. Think of a time when you felt on top of the world, like you just couldn't lose.
2. Now think of a different time when you felt totally carefree.
3. Now think of a different time when you had incredible fun.
4. With each instance, close your eyes and really associate with the memory. See what you saw, hear what you heard, and feel exactly the way you felt at the time. At the moment you most associate with that memory, pick up your coin and squeeze it in between your thumb and forefinger for a few seconds.
5. Take twenty seconds for each memory. First do 1. Then 2 and 3. Repeat if you want to really supercharge this feeling.

Carry that coin around with you this week. Put it in your pocket, or somewhere safe. It's simple, and effective.

> Every time you touch your coin with your thumb and forefinger, you're getting into Vegas Mode again. This is the NLP technique known as anchoring. And who knows what might happen next.

Remember, the research shows we can experiment with the way our brains experience the world, and anchoring is a useful NLP skill that you can have a lot of fun with.

> There are lots of studies to show how our brains struggle to differentiate between real experience and imagined experience. For example, experiments showed that people who repeatedly imagined eating a specific food (such as cheese) subsequently ate less of it than other people (2). They ate so much cheese in their imagination, they didn't want to eat it in reality any more.
>
> You can use anchoring to feel all sorts of different ways, or perhaps you'll just use it to eat less cheese.

Practice using anchors. See how they feel. Try using anchors to link positive thoughts and emotions to things you can see, hear, feel, smell or taste. That's what this *30 Day Expert* program is all about, learning and practicing every day. You could use anchoring to feel more motivated, more confident, on top of the world, or just get that winning feeling.

TO-DO LIST

- ☐ **Play around with anchoring thoughts and emotions.**
- ☐ **Get into "Vegas Mode" and see if it feels different. (It should.)**
- ☐ **Use anchoring to feel more inspired, confident, motivated, or even to eat less cheese.**

DAY 2

Get A Connection (But Don't Get The Sack)

> "Mirroring will make you feel awkward as heck when you first try it. That's the only hard part about it;."
>
> – Christopher Voss

In my career as a journalist, I once had a boss who was highly intimidating. For instance, he would put his feet up on his desk when he talked to me.

When I started learning NLP, I resolved to use the core technique of rapport to *match and mirror* his body language as much as possible. I didn't actually put my feet up on his desk. That clearly would have been a terrible idea. But one day, I forced myself to lean back in my chair to the same angle he was sitting at. This felt extraordinarily unnatural. I felt like a fraud. By mirroring his chair position I was almost tipping over.

Bizarrely though, the meeting was a success. It lasted over an hour and we seemed to connect. It finished with my boss saying, "Tony, I've enjoyed this. Come back anytime."

At the start of this 30 day program, we continue to cover some of the key concepts of NLP. And getting rapport is right at the top of the list. One of the best ways you can do this is by using mirroring (verbally, tonally and non-verbally).

Mirroring

This is the concept of "mirroring" somebody else's gestures. It's matching somebody else's body language (and potentially tonality and language structures too). As I leant back in my chair talking to my boss, I mirrored him, but subtly (same body position, same general vibe, but no feet on the desk, as that would have gone too far.)

> Mirroring makes us more convincing. Just take a look at the research.
>
> - Sales staff who mirrored their customers got more sales, and the customers liked them more (1).
> - In speed dating sessions, people who mirrored strangers for five minutes were rated more positively and seen as more attractive (2).
> - And research from Harvard showed "linguistic mirroring" made lawyers more persuasive (3).

Next time you're in a coffee shop or bar, look at some people who seem to get on particularly well. Study couples or friends who seem to have an easy rapport. (Don't stare – that would look strange.) Do they seem to mirror each other's body language? Are they talking in the same tone of voice, or at a similar rhythm? This is likely to be a good example of mirroring.

Now practice in communication with someone else. Here's what to do:

- Mirror their body language (subtly)
- Mirror their tonality (subtly)
- Mirror their language patterns (subtly)

Sometimes you can just mirror one thing rather than everything. Putting my feet up on the table when talking to my boss would have been inappropriate. But I was able to mirror his chair position.

Warning: Mirroring can unfortunately sometimes come across as a slightly hideous 80s body language business tip. Get this wrong and you may get caught out and look foolish. Mirror subtly. Don't do everything at once.

"As long as the mirroring is not weird."
– Charlene Eckstein

We do this mirroring with the best of intentions – to establish good rapport. Studies back up the power of rapport in almost every area. For example, make sure you get on well with your doctor, because positive rapport in healthcare is thought to lead to better treatment outcomes (4). Basically, if there is rapport, you are more likely to do what they say and get better quicker. Elsewhere, rapport skills in sales have "a tremendous impact on customer perceptions" (5).

> - Practice gently "mirroring" the movements of the people you find yourself with. Mirror their breathing patterns, body language, voice tone and posture. Mirror their language style – for example, do they swear a lot, or not at all? Do it subtly and sensitively.

It was well-known psychologist Professor Albert Mehrabian who originally said that 55% of our communication is non-verbal, 38% tonal (i.e., our tone of voice) and only 7% the actual words that we use). Many in the NLP world dispute that claim. But I think the 55% figure stands as a helpful metaphor for how important it is to focus on non-verbal communication and the words that we use. What we don't say is often even more important than what we say.

> **My best experience with mirroring**
>
> I had incredible success with this NLP skill when my son was a baby. He would often struggle to nap and was agitated with reflux and colic. So I would lay him on my chest, and very carefully mirror his breathing patterns. I would breathe at exactly the same pace as him, in time with him.
>
> It seemed to relax him (and me) and would eventually send him into a deep, sweet sleep. It was a beautiful experience and a lovely way to connect with my son.

NLP is all about communicating at your best with yourself and other people, and a key premise of these skills is to establish good rapport. Mirroring helps the other person feel a connection by noticing the similarities between you.

TO-DO LIST

- ☐ **Practice feeling a connection through mirroring.**
- ☐ **Mirror breathing patterns, body language, voice tone and language patterns.**
- ☐ **Be subtle (not weird).**

DAY 3

What Would You Love, Love, Love To Achieve?

> *"My goal in 2024 is to accomplish the goals I set in 2023 which I should have done in 2022 because I made a promise in 2021 which I planned in 2020."*
>
> – Unknown

Neuro-Linguistic Programming is often linked to success and high performance. And that's why goal-setting and "getting stuff done" comes early in this book.

There is some compelling science on goal-setting, but right at the start of Day 3, I want to emphasize that it's crucial that your goals should be achievable. In other words, don't expect to be a millionaire by Friday and then complain to me that the NLP goal-setting doesn't work.

Here's what you want to go for: your NLP outcomes should feel like a stretch, but not too much of a stretch. Dr. Edwin Locke and Dr. Gary Latham reviewed a number of studies on goal-setting and found that difficult goals help us succeed, as long as they're not too difficult.

"In 90% of the studies, specific and challenging goals led to higher performance than easy goals, "do your best" goals, or no goals. Goals affect performance by directing attention, mobilizing effort, increasing persistence and motivating strategy development" (1).

Goals, Outcomes and HUGGs

The first point to make is that, in NLP **we turn goals into "outcomes"**. This projects us firmly forward into the reality of actually getting stuff done.

Write Your Outcome

So you have a realistic goal in mind? Let's NLP it and turn it into an outcome.

- Can you express your goal succinctly?
- Make sure this goal is possible and attainable.
- Turn it into an outcome by *saying it in the present as if it's already happened.*
- Focus on what you will feel when you've completed it.
- Write it down in 15 words or fewer.
- Date it with the day on which you'll be completing it.

Example:

Outcome:

I use NLP every day now that I've finished this program. It feels great!

29th March

HUGGs

HUGGs are the opposite of our NLP outcomes. It means Huge Unbelievably Great Goals. Having something important, exciting and meaningful to work towards is extremely motivating. But these need to be approached in the right way. HUGGs with no plan will wither and die. Have you ever watched the film *The Secret*? It was inspiring. The Law of Intention is powerful. But it isn't the case that solely by thinking something, it'll happen.

HUGGs are important and they provide a guiding star and motivation for what we want to achieve. What I like is combining Huge Unbelievably Great Goals with small victories to actually make them happen.

> **GOAL-SETTING THEORY**
>
> My podcast *Zestology* explores all sorts of health, wellness and NLP-related topics. Over the past decade, there is one guest who has been on more than any other: my friend Dr. Stephen Simpson. He is a well-known Creative Mind and Performance Coach, and we met on an NLP training course almost 20 years ago.
>
> We have made it a tradition to record New Year's Day podcasts on goals and outcomes. While we love using outcomes, over the years we've tried every approach there is. Dr. Stephen even once presented a prestigious talk in front of 400 people, with no end goal at all, but with the *intention* of delivering an outstanding talk that would enthuse and interest his audience. Predictably, they loved it. It just shows there are lots of different ways to approach outcomes.

Creating HUGGs

- Think about goals: ones that almost seem too big to comprehend right now; creating something that positively affects lots of people. It might be a huge promotion that you're a long way away from, running a marathon, or similar.
- In the same way as we have done with outcomes, write it down and date it as if it's happened.
- As we are talking HUGGs, this might be 5, 10 or 20 years in the future.

Making Goals Happen

> *"The great victory, which appears so simple today, was the result of a series of small victories that went unnoticed."*
>
> – Paulo Coelho

Now come the small victories.

> ➤ Whether your goal is to be achieved one month, one year, or three decades in the future, break it down into smaller chunks. Depending on how long it is, start by year, then go by month and then by day. What do you need to do tomorrow to take you one tiny step closer to your big goal?

It's all very well doing as Bruce Lee did. He wrote a letter to himself in 1969 telling himself he would be the "best known oriental movie star in the United States" and would make $10 million. If he'd just written the letter and done nothing else about it, he probably wouldn't have been one of the best known movie stars 10 years later. What actually got him there was all the hard work, day to day grind, craft, training and learning.

To achieve his goal, he used Huge Unbelievably Great Goals. But he also focused on small victories. This is my favorite part of goal-setting. It is about focusing on the process.

When I made the transition from radio to TV presenter, I really wanted the job. I felt like my career was going stale and I needed a change. There was one channel that I particularly wanted to work on – one of the UK's most popular TV stations. After 18 months of trying, I finally managed to get a screen test. It seemed like a long shot – I would be trying out alongside 60 other people that day.

> **NLP AND GOAL-SETTING RESEARCH**
>
> A study on athletes showed how effective NLP goal-setting tools are. The athletes (all expert shooters) found that NLP techniques improved their scores in both ordinary conditions and under pressure.
>
> "Small victories" were the key – setting big outcomes and breaking them down into smaller, more achievable goals.
>
> *The participants of the present study learned the principles of goal-setting in NLP such as how to break goals down into several smaller, short-term goals and achieve them accurately based on their own capabilities. (2)*

The day I found out I had a screen test for my dream TV journalist job. I wrote my outcomes. I dated them in the present. And then I set about all the small victories I needed in order to make it happen; the autocue practice, the knowledge, the house style, even the right haircut and a new suit. Five months later, almost to the day, I started my first presenting shift at my new job. That was HUGGs in action, and it couldn't have happened without all the small victories that got me there. Or maybe it was just the new haircut…

TO-DO LIST

- ☐ **Set some "outcomes" to get stuff done.**
- ☐ **Create some HUGGs. Aim big. These are the fun ones.**
- ☐ **Finally, focus on the process. How will you actually achieve these goals?**

DAY 4

Communicate (A Bit) Better

Paula and her partner argued non-stop. When they'd first met each other, they seemed the perfect match. But over the years, they'd drifted apart. A quick glance at their messages showed you how bad things were. "Look, it's clear that you simply can't see my point of view here," she would write. "How hard is it for you to grasp? I just feel so low," her partner would reply.

We experience the world with our five senses: sight, sound, touch, smell and taste. You'll find the senses referred to repeatedly over the next 30 days because a key part of NLP is tapping into each individual's unique sensory blueprint.

The senses we use are called Representational Systems. And, believe it or not, understanding these sensory modalities better is key to unlocking communication with other people and ourselves.

When I started to learn this, I immediately felt I started to communicate a bit better (hence Day 4's title). It wasn't earth-shattering, but a subtle improvement in the way I got on with people that improved over time. And then understanding this concept helped me to improve at the more advanced NLP techniques too.

Paula used lots of visual language (look, clear, see, view) and her partner favored physical, touchy-feely language (hard, grasp, feel). The result was a communication mis-match.

Senses (Representational Systems)

The five senses are:

- Visual (what we see)
- Auditory (what we hear)
- Kinesthetic (what we touch and feel)
- Olfactory (what we smell)
- Gustatory (what we taste)

Preferences

> *"I'm a visual thinker, not a language-based thinker. My brain is like Google Images."*
>
> – Temple Grandin

Some people have a preferred representational system. That means they have a sense they favor over others. I'm also very visual, so the way something looks might be more important to me than the way it feels.

And this was the problem with Paula and her partner, as we saw above: (Paula – visual, and partner – kinesthetic.)

When you can work out what sense or senses somebody else favors, you can use this to get on with them (and consequently improve your communication) much more quickly and successfully. It's not about "getting your way", but making things better for both of you.

Thus, we come back to the importance of rapport, and matching that we looked at on Day 2. Today, let's establish rapport by matching language and appreciating the representational systems that we and other people use.

> Play with matching your language to a partner/friend/colleague. Work out how they experience the world and what their preferred representational system is. Then use words that match it, whether it's visual ("seeing things their way"), auditory ("hearing what they are saying"), or kinesthetic ("getting to grips with how they feel").

Note – it's rare that somebody's preferred representational system would be smelling or tasting.

Paula worked on matching her language to her partner's – both in messages and in person. She talked about her feelings and noticed when her partner did the same. This helped. They had been experiencing the world through different lenses. As they tuned into each other's preferred representational system, they developed a better understanding of each other.

The Mysterious Sixth Sense

There are actually six representational systems in NLP. Five of them relate to the senses. The sixth is called Auditory Digital – it isn't related to a specific sense but to internal dialogue, facts, figures and logic.

People who are very "auditory digital" might have a strong preference for logic, facts, figures and order. They love a spreadsheet or a flow chart.

Tuning into the world

By switching on our senses, we can communicate better with ourselves and others. We can be more loving and kinder in our relationships. We can tune in to the needs of others and be more persuasive when we need to be.

By being aware of representational systems and keeping our senses wide open, we can play with how we experience the world.

In this book, you'll experience many NLP approaches based on the senses.

- We can make pictures more vivid and colorful when we want to associate more closely with a memory.
- We can "turn the sound down" on our pesky internal voice or imposter syndrome.
- We might want to use the power of touch to help us feel a different way (see the anchored coin from Day 1).

One more point on senses. In *Stop Scrolling*, I wrote about "Scroller Steve" who sits on the toilet, checking his emails while simultaneously cleaning his teeth, cutting his nails and listening to a podcast. While this might be extreme, our screens take us away from actually experiencing the world and using our full range of sensory awareness.

Just on email alone – some workers have been observed to check their email over 400 times a day, and on average, three working hours per day are being lost to email. If we do that, then how can we notice a bird tweeting, a slight change in air temperature or our partner's subtle change in mood when our focus is so narrow?

The trick is to switch off, and tune into our senses. There is more on playing around with the senses tomorrow.

TO-DO LIST

- ☐ Talk to a friend. Work out what representational system they prefer.
- ☐ Match it when you are with them. Communicate (a bit) better.
- ☐ Remember, this is not about "getting your way", but understanding each other better.

DAY 5

Improve Your Memory, Eyesight & Brainpower

> "My brain is like the Bermuda Triangle, information goes in and then it is never found again."
>
> – Unknown

If there was something you could do right now, something that science has proven improves your speed of movement, dexterity, blood pressure, eyesight, memory and cognitive abilities, would you do it? It's all related to the NLP concept you will learn today.

Can Mindset Help Us Delay Aging?

Award-winning psychologist Dr. Ellen Langer carried out a famous experiment on a process that she found led to better health, optimism and vitality amongst elderly men. It involved them feeling younger and healthier simply by changing the way they thought and acted.

A group of men in their late 70s and 80s were told to pretend to be the person they had been 20 years earlier. From the moment they walked through the doors of the experiment, they acted and were treated as if they were younger. They had to do hard physical tasks themselves, and then be measured against a control group. They "watched films, listened to music from the time and had discussions about Castro marching on Havana and a NASA satellite launch – all in the present tense." (1)

The men improved across the board and against a control group. Their gait, dexterity, arthritis, speed of movement, cognitive abilities and memory were all measurably improved. Incredibly, tests also showed that their eyesight got better and their hearing improved.

Because they were thinking younger, their bodies followed suit.

Association and Dissociation

This experiment elegantly shows the power of the NLP core concepts of association and dissociation.

Perhaps the secret ingredient for living your best life is simply deeply associating with how you want to be as a person.

There are so many things we can't control in life. But we can control our behavior, and when we do that effectively, our behavior can propel us towards our goals.

Dr. Ellen Langer's subjects did that, successfully associating with such improvements in their lives, and living that way.

> **CAN YOU SEE BETTER THAN YOU THINK?**
>
> Dr. Ellen Langer has done a ton of research on how your mindset can affect our vision. Here are three fascinating examples.
>
> - Participants were told that people who exercise have better eyesight, and then they started working out. As they exercised more, their vision improved because they believed it would.
> - When people pretended to be pilots and flew on a simulator, their vision got better.
> - People were asked to look at a reversed eye chart (where the letters went from small to big). They were able to see letters they couldn't see before. Why? Langer found their mindset was different because of the changed chart (2).

But frustratingly, we often associate with the bad stuff – failures, shortcomings, worries – and dissociate from ourselves at our very best – focused, witty, intelligent, healthy, etc.

Practice Association

This exercise is about looking forward rather than Dr. Langer's exercise on looking back. But it follows the same premise.

> ➢ Associate with exactly how you'd like to be at the end of this 30 day program. Identify who and where you want to be, put yourself in the picture, and make it big, bright and vivid. Make the sounds loud and clear, and notice how good it feels as you truly associate with your best self.

If your goal is to become a world class piano player, then associate with the way you want to be. It may be you at your most studious, fit, healthy, focused, curious, or something else. Associate with mental imagery of you at your best.

Practice Dissociation

So far we've focused more on association, but dissociation is one of the most powerful NLP concepts.

So, think of something that makes you feel anxious or worried. Practice at first on something small, rather than a huge, traumatic life event. Create a mental picture in your mind that represents this. It might be a memory or a nagging worry. (You can always return to the more challenging topics as you master these skills.)

- See this thing/event as if you are watching yourself in the third person (the first bit of dissociation).
- Now we alter the "submodalities" of the mental picture. First, change the picture from color to black and white.
- Reduce the clarity and size of the picture.
- Gradually push the picture further away.

- Turn the sound down.
- Make it muffled and unclear.
- Finally, move your third person self even further away as you watch yourself.

This is dissociation. How does this area of your life now make you feel? Does it have less emotional impact?

> **SUBMODALITIES**
>
> Submodalities is one of those jargony terms you will hear a lot in NLP. It refers to the textures of what we experience through our senses – what we are seeing, hearing or feeling.
>
> It's the difference between color and black-and-white, near and far, or warm and cool. And with tools like association and dissociation, we can play around with these submodalities to change the way we feel.
>
> "The change of submodalities can have a strong effect on other submodalities, even in another sense. For example, if you increase the brightness of an image in our minds, that intensity could increase the sensations it determines" (3).

TO-DO LIST

- ☐ Use association to improve your mindset (or your eyesight).
- ☐ Experiment with dissociation to feel less anxious or worried.
- ☐ Remember, this is all about submodalities (the textures of the senses).

DAY 6

In Praise Of Variety

I have suffered from some frustrating stomach issues over the years. I first started experiencing gut-related symptoms when I was 18. Having previously been in good health, I began to develop digestive problems. These were initially just unpleasant. I'd have low energy the day after a few drinks with my buddies (beer was the worst), or eating a pizza. Over the years, the lows got worse and I'd feel sluggish, sick, and anxious.

So I embarked on a mission and tried everything to sort it out. At various times over the past two decades, I've given up gluten, dairy, soy, peanuts and indeed every type of nut. I've been on high-carb diets, low-carb diets and even the keto diet for a year and a half. I've read (what felt like) hundreds of books. Finally, after 25 years of testing different diets, I stumbled upon a niche concept that changed my life for the better. And in fact it was a Neuro-Linguistic Programming principle that had helped me get to that point and turn my health around.

Presuppositions

NLP has several basic principles that we "presuppose" to be true. These are called "presuppositions". We're going to focus for two days on these, starting with an important one.

The Law Of Requisite Variety

The more variety you can introduce into your life, the more you can adjust and operate at your best.

The Law of Requisite Variety is worth respecting on your route to NLP expertise. It means you should be as open-minded and flexible as possible. It tells us that when we're doing something that isn't working, we should try something else. Or to put it another way:

We're going to apply this law to 1) our life and then 2) our NLP journey. First, here's how you could apply The Law of Requisite Variety to just about anything in your life today.

> The Law of Requisite Variety can best be described as a state of curiosity. So today, be curious. Try new things. Eat new foods. Ride a tandem. (Okay, maybe that's too much.) The law tells us the more variety you can introduce into your life, the more you can adjust and operate at your best.

CULTIVATE INTENSE CURIOSITY

Leonardo Da Vinci seemed to be fascinated by just about everything. He embraced curiosity. He would write in his notebook on mechanics, the flow of rivers, astronomy, optics, architecture, the flight of birds… anything that interested him.

We know this because over 7,000 pages of his notebooks have survived today, stuffed with notes, drawings, diagrams, pictures, inventions and ideas. They can be found in the British Library. (1)

He's a good example of the Law of Requisite Variety. He sought out (an intense amount of) variety in order to operate at his best. And he left an important legacy as a painter, engineer, scientist, theorist, sculptor, and architect.

How The Law of Requisite Variety has helped me

Back to my stomach issues. After years of testing different diets, I stumbled upon a niche concept that changed my life for the better. It was called a low histamine diet.

This was one of the most complicated diets to understand (for example: avocados and tomatoes = bad, apples and celery = good). Remarkably, within a few hours of following a low histamine diet, I felt a bit better. Almost instantly, my symptoms improved. Was I imagining it? No. I continued to improve and in fact I still follow it now. I have even written a book about this diet. It has been life changing. And I only discovered it because I followed The Law of Requisite Variety. The more variety I introduced, the more I honed in on the problem. Admittedly it took a long time, but thank goodness I knew about this presupposition. It's changed my life.

"The definition of insanity is doing the same thing over and over again and expecting a different result."

– Attributed to Albert Einstein

The second reason I wanted to focus on this law is that it is a helpful presupposition for learning NLP. There is a rich selection of techniques in this book. Perhaps the key is just to try lots of them.

- Be curious about all the NLP skills in this book.
- Don't be wedded to one type of technique, genre of book, teacher or anything.
- Give yourself and other people choices. The more variety you introduce, the more you will be able to succeed.

What I like best about this presupposition is that it encourages you to question everything, even the principles in this book. You might enjoy this book, and then read another book on CBT or EFT and find that even more helpful.

The Law of Requisite Variety says… that's wonderful.

LEARNING ABOUT PRESUPPOSITIONS

NLP has lots of these "presuppositions". These are basic principles that we "presuppose" to be true, and the Law of Requisite Variety is one of them. Others include;

- *The map is not the territory* (reality is different from our perception of it. We will look more at this presupposition tomorrow).
- *Behind every behavior there is a positive intention* (for example, somebody smokes because it helps them relax, or feel more social, even if they know it is bad for their health).
- *There is no failure, only feedback* (this does what it says on the tin, and is related to the Law of Requisite Variety).

TO-DO LIST

- ☐ **Use The Law of Requisite Variety to be flexible and operate at your best.**
- ☐ **Consider which areas of your life you could try new stuff in.**
- ☐ **Be curious. That's what The Law of Requisite Variety and NLP are all about.**

DAY 7

Don't Trust The GPS

Me and my friend John were on holiday in Argentina. We wanted to visit a little town rated as one of the most beautiful places on the edge of the desert and the Andes. The town was called Barreal, and it was in the middle of nowhere. But we didn't have much money to get there. So we hired the cheapest car we could find (a beaten-up old red Volkswagen Gol), put Barreal into the GPS, and set off. What could possibly go wrong?

After a while, something weird happened. As we started driving through the desert, the road just ended. It vanished. We went from a normal tarmac road to some stones. And all the traffic seemed to disappear too. We passed two cars in three hours.

Perhaps we should have known better. Barreal is really quite remote. If you take the southern route out of Mendoza, you hit the desert. We should have taken the northern route. But the sat-nav had sent us south.

Our phone reception disappeared. We started to get nervous. This car was not built for driving across a desert with no road. Then... we got a flat tire.

Did we have a spare? John jumped out to check. We did! Amazing. Somehow we managed to fix the tire and get back on the road. But we were lucky. If we hadn't had a spare, we'd have been stranded in the desert with no phone reception, no road and night-time fast approaching.

That tire is properly flat. Argentina, 2009.

Chastened, we clambered back into the car and I drove at 20mph for the next five hours to ensure we didn't get another flat before Barreal. I'd been reminded of a valuable NLP principle.

The Map Is Not The Territory

It may sound obvious, but just because the map shows a road through the desert, that doesn't necessarily mean the road exists. The map is not the territory. Duh. I should have remembered my NLP training.

I'm not the first person to have made this sort of mistake. Did you ever hear about;

- The holidaymakers who drove into the sea?
- The poor couple who went to Carpi rather than Capri?
- The driver who followed instructions from her GPS and ended up stranded on the roof of her car in a swamp?

All of them would have benefited from learning about presuppositions and Day 7's important NLP principle.

The map is not the territory

The way we see the world is not the world itself. It has gone through a series of deletions, distortions and generalizations to arrive at this "reality." And the same goes for our internal map of the world.

Today, let's reconnect our internal GPS, and spot any differences between the *map* and the *territory*. Take a moment to consider the NLP presupposition, *the map is not the territory*. Just because the GPS tells you to drive into a swamp, it doesn't mean that's the right thing to do.

EPIC GPS FAIL

Japanese tourists in Australia took a seriously wrong turn because of their GPS. It somehow forgot that there is nine miles of water between North Stradbroke Island and mainland Australia. So they drove into the Pacific Ocean.

50 yards in, they realized their mistake. They tried to turn back but they were in too deep. The tide forced them to abandon the car, but thankfully they were able to get back to shore unharmed.

"It told us we could drive down there," Yuzu Noda, 21, told the local newspaper. "It kept saying it would navigate us to a road. We got stuck… there's lots of mud." (1)

Another reminder that the map is not the territory.

> Pick a goal that you are working towards, and then ask yourself some questions about it: "Where do I want to go? What is the fastest route there? Am I following the correct directions? Do I need to change course, or find an alternative route? Do I need a new map?"

We look at the same pictures but we see different things. Sometimes, the map just isn't right. Sometimes we get so involved in the busy-ness of life, we forget to stop and consider whether we're actually going in the right direction. Sometimes, we need to redraw our maps and remap our internal representation of the world.

For now, it's only important that you remember the map is not the territory. This concept will pop up repeatedly over the next month.

"Reality is merely an illusion, albeit a very persistent one."
– Albert Einstein

TO-DO LIST

- ☐ **Ask yourself: Where do I want to go?**
- ☐ **Think about your route there. Are you following the correct directions?**
- ☐ **Do you need to change course, or redraw your map of the world?**

DAY 8

Counting Chimneys

In *Stop Scrolling*, I looked at the work of Professor Andrew Huberman, who says the simple act of looking upwards sends a wakefulness signal to the brain. This is down to the connection between brain stem circuits and other neural circuits that control wakefulness.

He recommends raising your eyes and holding that gaze for 15 seconds to feel more alert, and conversely looking downwards if you want to feel more sleepy (1).

The neural connections between our eyes and the way we think and feel are fascinating. One of the things the NLP pioneers showed right from the start is that you could look at where someone's eyes were looking and – generally speaking, but not always – it would tell a bit about what they are thinking.

> *"If people could read my mind, I'd get punched in the face a lot."*
>
> – Unknown

Eye Accessing Cues

This is a fun one, so it often comes at the start of NLP training. In my experience it works for about 90% of people around 90% of the time. It's not something I use on a day to day basis, but it's always something that people are interested in. "Oh, I can find out if my partner's lying to me. Tell me more about that!" That sort of thing.

So the idea is that when you look at someone;

- If they look upwards and to the right (as you look at them), then they are remembering something. (So you can remember it this way: right and remembered.)
- If they look level to the right, they are remembering something auditory (sounds).
- If they look downwards and to the right, they are accessing their internal dialogue (auditory digital).
- If they look up and to the left, then they're constructing something visual.
- If they look level and to the left, they're constructing something auditory.
- If they are looking downwards and to the left, they are accessing feelings and thoughts.

That's the basic premise. I personally don't prioritize spending my entire life looking at where people's eyes are going but this is still useful information for a number of reasons.

Here's how you could use eye-accessing cues in the real world.

1. If you or your clients meditate, this might be interesting. With your eyes open or closed, make sure you are looking upwards. That way, according to NLP principles, you find it much harder to access your internal dialogue and (potentially negative) feelings.
2. *Mind Factor* founder Karl Morris uses this tip with top sports star clients when things aren't going their way. We tend to look down when we are processing thoughts and feelings. So he encourages them to look up. It gets us out of our heads and into our senses. Note: I find this helpful myself and often use it.

3. Legend has it that the famous hypnotherapist Dr. Milton Erickson used to get his depressed patients to count chimney pots for the same reason. By looking up, they escaped "feeling low" and their inner dialogue.
4. Want to know if someone is lying? See if their eyes are looking to the left. According to eye accessing cues this would indicate they are "constructing" something. However, it might also just indicate they are looking over to the left. Which is why you always want to look for groups of signs with body language.

What about the science?

As you know by now, I like to refer to the science. And eye-accessing cues are, er, a bit of an outlier. It's not to say that the science doesn't exist, but there are "difficulties". Andy Smith, my first NLP trainer, has tackled this issue in depth. In 2013 he said, "eye accessing cues are a favorite target for 'skeptics' wishing to 'debunk' NLP." As Andy notes, there are all sorts of difficulties in "designing experiments that adequately test the hypothesis" (2).

However, new research is beginning to emerge. Three experiments were carried out on students at the University of Geneva to investigate whether there is a link between gaze direction and verbal processing of various tasks. The results suggested looking up during verbal tasks would be beneficial (3).

My own view is that many of the elements of NLP are backed up by strong science, but more research is needed into eye-accessing cues. There are, however, links between eye position and neural cues that are worth exploring.

TO-DO LIST

- ☐ **Notice eye-accessing cues when having conversations.**
- ☐ **Try looking upwards for a quick state change. It works for top sports stars.**
- ☐ **Don't rely solely on eye-accessing cues. Combine them with your other NLP skills.**

DAY 9

Change Your Perspective

> *"In your mind, change the name of every day to Saturday. And change the name of work to play."*
>
> – Matt Haig, from The Humans

An NLP reframe is simply when you change your perspective on something. You may have looked at the title of this mini-chapter and thought, "sounds pretty simple". I guess it is. But reframes work. Once you perceive something differently, your behavior can change, too. A problem can become an opportunity. And Mondays feel like Saturdays.

Reframes

My friend recently said to me, "This weather's bad. I get depressed when summer ends."

Is that you? Do you feel a bit down when the hot weather disappears? If so, do a "reframe" by writing a list of five things you love about autumn.

I'm writing this in October. The leaves are beginning to fall. So here is my list.

- autumnal walks
- the leaves changing color
- the football season

- winter cooking and a warming roast dinner ("Yorkshire Puddings", one of the greatest inventions ever!)
- log fires

That's it. I have reframed autumn by changing my perspective. Sure I'd still like to be lounging by the pool in the middle of high summer, but now I'm feeling a little bit better about autumn too.

"Autumn leaves don't fall, they fly. They take their time and wander on this, their only chance to soar."

– Delia Owens, *Where The Crawdads Sing*

Some people see dead leaves and others see something else. A reframe can gently, or sometimes powerfully, change the way we think about things.

> ### FROM DEATH CAMP TO EXISTENTIALISM
>
> This was the original title of Victor Frankl's book (later issued as *Man's Search for Meaning*), in which he reframed his experience in a concentration camp. To me, this is perhaps the ultimate reframe, to take the most horrific of circumstances and find meaning. This beautiful, inspiring book is a must-read.
>
> Frankl lost everything except one thing: "*...the last of the human freedoms, to choose one's attitude in any given set of circumstances, to choose one's own way.*"
>
> He said some prisoners were able to find meaning in their lives despite horrific conditions. He kept his mind active by planning lectures on what he wanted to teach. This, Frankl says, allowed him to move forward and survive the death camp (1) (2).

Blips, hiccups and glitches

In NLP we think deeply about the language we use. Here's another example of why.

I like the word blip. It implies that everything will be fine, and that this is just a small, temporary setback. It's just an insignificant hiccup on the road to success.

Why am I talking about blips? Here's my point. I got ill many years ago. I went to the jungle and contracted a virus. Afterwards, I suffered from post-viral fatigue. Someone wise told me when I was feeling bad I should view it as a blip, not a nightmare. I loved that, and it changed how I thought about the times when I wasn't feeling 100%.

> ➢ How can you reframe some of your self-talk? There's a big difference between a hiccup and a cock-up, or a glitch and a meltdown.

Pick something you don't feel good about, and try to change the way you talk to yourself about it.

"It's snowing still," said Eeyore gloomily.
"So it is."
"And freezing."
"Is it?"
"Yes," said Eeyore. "However," he said, brightening up a little, "we haven't had an earthquake lately."

– A.A.Milne

TO-DO LIST

- ☐ Find some things in your life to reframe.
- ☐ Practice reframing "cock ups" into "hiccup"'.
- ☐ Use reframes whenever you need to change state. They can gently, or sometimes powerfully, change how we think.

DAY 10

How To Learn To Play Bach's Concerto In D

Would you like to be able to play Bach's Concerto In D? Today I'll show you how, using NLP.

First, though, I need to be completely honest with you. It may not surprise you to hear that this process will not be easy. However, it is possible.

Modeling

Modeling might be the most important NLP skill. By observing and sometimes replicating the ways others achieve results, we can start to learn from them and improve ourselves.

Let's start Day 10 by focusing on actress Meryl Streep. Her powers of modeling are legendary. When preparing for the role of violinist in a film called *Music of the Heart*, as always, she wanted to be as authentic as possible. She dedicated herself to the role so completely that she learned and practiced the violin for six hours a day over the course of two months. She immersed herself in someone else's skills (violinist Roberta Guaspari, on whom her role was based).

That's dedication.

At the end of it she could play... you guessed it, Bach's Concerto In D. Apparently even now she is proud of the effort she put in, and the enjoyment she got from achieving a new skill. She devotes her undivided attention to the task of succeeding in a role. She is an expert modeler, and her record 21 Oscar nominations bear witness to this.

> *"I'm curious about other people. That's the essence of my acting. I'm interested in what it would be like to be you."*
>
> – Meryl Streep

Incidentally, Streep didn't just model Roberta Guasperi's violin-playing. She modeled her personality, mannerisms and speaking voice so successfully that film critic Roger Ebert wrote;

"Meryl Streep is known for her mastery of accents; she may be the most versatile speaker in the movies…. This is not Streep's voice, but someone else's – with a certain flat quality, as if later education and refinement came after a somewhat unsophisticated childhood."

NLP Modeling

- Identify someone who has skills, achievements or successes that you would like to replicate in some way.
- It can be somebody famous, somebody well known in their field, or someone you know personally.
- Approach them if you can, and ask questions about their <u>environment</u>, <u>behavior</u>, <u>capabilities</u>, <u>values</u>, <u>beliefs</u> or <u>identity</u>.
- If you can't approach them, read about them and study them, asking the same kinds of questions.
- Consider how you can apply the relevant learnings to your life. You're not copying, but learning from experts.

> ### A PERSONAL EXPERIENCE OF MODELING
>
> I love taking inspiration on being creative from all sorts of unusual directions, both at the day-to-day level (behavior), and the big stuff too (values and beliefs)
>
> I'm currently obsessed with legendary music producer Rick Rubin. He's worked with everybody from Run DMC to Metallica, so there's a lot to learn about his creative process.
>
> First I modeled a <u>behavior</u> of Rick Rubin's – he meditates every morning, and that has helped me. But it's also helped me to know about his <u>values</u> too. Here's one little example. *"Focus on something you love, because you have a far greater chance of succeeding by doing something you love, and regardless of whether you succeed or not, your life will be better. So you can't really lose by dedicating yourself to what you love"* (1).
>
> Learning about high achievers at a <u>values</u>, <u>beliefs</u>, and <u>identity</u> level is often where the real magic of modeling takes place.

At the start of this mini-chapter I promised to explain how you can learn to play Bach's Concerto In D. The answer is to model the modeler. Model Meryl Streep (who in turn modeled violinist Roberta Guaspari), and study her <u>environment</u>, <u>behavior</u>, <u>capabilities</u>, <u>values</u>, <u>beliefs</u> and <u>identity</u>.

So how can you "do a Meryl"? What would happen if you gave your goal six hours a day of dedication?

None of us have all of the answers. That's why modeling is so powerful. We can always learn from others.

TO-DO LIST

- ☐ Find somebody you'd like to model with NLP, famous or otherwise.
- ☐ Model their environment, behavior, capabilities, values, beliefs and identity.
- ☐ Take inspiration. Apply what you've learnt to your own life.

DAY 11

Throw Out The Alarm Clock

My Mum has never used an alarm clock. When she wants to wake up at, say, 7am, she taps her head on the pillow seven times before she goes to sleep. This has always amazed me. How on earth can it work? When I've got an early start I need three iPhone alarms just to wake up.

She told me lots of people in her generation used to do this, and it turns out that her unusual alarm clock strategy may be backed up by science.

For three nights, a team at the University of Lubeck in Germany put volunteers to bed at midnight. They were all woken at 6am (ouch). But while some were expecting it, others had been told they'd get a lie in til 9am. The results tell us a lot about the unconscious processes going on in our bodies.

- The group <u>expecting</u> to wake early had a significant rise in stress hormones from 4.30am, peaking around 6am.
- People woken <u>unexpectedly</u> at 6am had no such spike in stress hormones.

The unconscious mind, the researchers concluded, keeps track of time while we sleep and sets a sort of biological alarm clock (1). Almost certainly, that's what's going on with my Mum's pillow ritual.

The Unconscious Mind

Your brain has a massive "hard drive." (Excuse the computer terminology – it kind of works though). It can hold a huge amount of information but can't access it all at once. It can only consciously think of a few things at the same time. But our unconscious mind can do all sorts of things "beneath the hood", including preparing us to wake up while we are still asleep.

We refer to this in Neuro-Linguistic Programming as the difference between the conscious mind, and the "unconscious mind", which deals with all the things on the hard drive that just whir away in the background – like breathing. Imagine if you had to remember to breathe every time.

> *"Ninety-five percent of thought, emotion, and learning occur in the unconscious mind that is, without our awareness"*
>
> *– Gerald Zaltman*

It is said that the conscious mind can only think of around seven things (plus or minus two) at once. The unconscious mind looks after everything else.

Want an example of this? Think about blinking. Focus on your own blinking. Straightaway, you are now conscious of your blinking. But for the whole of the rest of the day, you probably haven't thought about blinking once. That means the activity of blinking has moved from your unconscious mind to becoming one of the things you are now thinking about with your conscious mind.

This concept of the unconscious mind will pop up again and again, which is why it's so important to learn about it today.

- ➢ Remember this concept of the unconscious mind. In all sorts of techniques coming up (chunking, affirmations, hypnosis and more), we look to learn effectively at a conscious level so that it becomes unconscious. In NLP, that's called "unconscious competence".

> "The Magical Number Seven"
>
> To learn a little bit more about the difference between the conscious mind and the unconscious mind, we can turn to the work of psychologist George Miller. He wrote a famous paper in 1965 on our short-term memory. He showed it is severely limited in terms of the amount of information it can receive, process, and remember. He found seven "plus or minus two things" in our mind is the magic number (2).
>
> So if somebody tells you their phone number, you might remember it, but if they tell you their credit card number, you might struggle. The theory goes that there would be too many bits of information for your conscious mind to handle at once.

Fun exercise

This unconscious mind works away while we sleep (hence our dreams) and we can give it a little nudge in the right direction.

- Pick an area where you feel a little stuck. Perhaps it's an issue at work, or a goal that you haven't made much progress on.
- Before you drop off tonight, ask your "unconscious mind" to think about three instances where you can take action.
- Do nothing else. Just go to sleep. Allow your mind's hard drive to work away in the background.
- As the days and weeks pass, notice if you instinctively take more action in the chosen area.

Admittedly, this method requires a small leap of faith, as it is unconventional to talk to yourself like this. But it is a good way to tune in to the power of the unconscious mind.

TO-DO LIST

- ☐ Tune into the difference between your conscious and unconscious mind.
- ☐ Start to trust your unconscious mind to come up with some answers.
- ☐ Just for fun, ditch the alarm clock and try the "pillow-tap" instead.

DAY 12

Chunking Up and Chunking Down

Following on from yesterday's adventures with the unconscious mind, let's do something related—NLP "chunking".

In simple terms, chunking refers to the level of detail you are thinking at. Think of it as "zooming out or zooming in" on a particular topic.

- **Chunking up** helps us zoom out to see the whole picture by understanding how the parts come together. It helps us to think strategically.
- **Chunking down** helps us zoom in, and become precise as we go into the detail. It helps us to think forensically.

Chunking

> "Great things are not done by impulse, but by a series of small things brought together."
> – Van Gogh

The tiniest things you do in pursuit of your goal (for example: each brush stroke/paint color etc) relate to the biggest things (outcome: finished painting). And we can chunk up and down by asking good questions.

Here's a chunking exercise for you to try.

- Pick a goal or outcome: something you'd like to achieve.

- **Chunk down.** Zoom in to understand the detail (small chunks) required to achieve your big goal?
- Ask questions like; what is an example of this? What/where/how specifically?
- Continue to chunk down into as much detail as you like.
- **Now chunk up.** Look at each chunk and ask; how does this fit into my plan? What purpose does it have? How do the parts relate to the whole?
- How high can you chunk, and how wide can you zoom out to find the ultimate purpose in what you are doing?

HOW SPECIFICALLY WILL YOU USE CHUNKING?

I like the concept of The Law Of Attraction. This is the philosophy that positive thoughts bring positive results. But it's no good pinning a note to your fridge declaring you want a new job, and not doing anything else to actually get it.

You need to chunk down. Once you come up with the big goal, you need to ask yourself some good questions to get into what is required. A particularly good question for chunking down is "how specifically?"

- BIg chunk: I want a new job.
- *How specifically are you going to get it?*
- Smaller chunk – I start applying for jobs.
- *How specifically?*
- Smaller chunk – I write my CV and send it out.
- *How specifically?*
- Smaller chunk – I ask friends for advice on layout and content.
- *How specifically?*
- Smaller chunk – I open my laptop and send a message.
- And so on…

Let's look at another example. I will now take a massive liberty and imagine how Van Gogh's creative process might have worked. Considering I was consistently bottom of the class at art, this could be interesting.

- Van Gogh decides to paint a scene (big chunk)
- Thinks deeply about style and what colors (smaller chunk)
- Considers which part of the artwork to paint first (smaller chunk)
- Decides which color to paint first (smaller chunk)
- Decides which brush to use (smaller chunk)
- Steps back to see how each stroke relates to the strategy (bigger chunk)
- Asks if each individual stroke and color is creating the desired big picture (bigger chunk)
- Asks if his overall vision is being achieved or does he need to correct course (big chunk)
- And so on

Obviously I've taken a huge amount of creative license here in imagining Van Gogh's process. But it's easy to imagine that Van Gogh was good at **chunking up** (thinking strategically about "great things" like a finished painting) *and* **chunking down** (thinking forensically about paint, use of color, style, composition and brush strokes).

Further examples

What we do over the long term with **chunking up** is take lots of information and put it together into one easily accessible mental file. Let's look at two very different professions – chess grandmaster and surgeon.

> *"If you compare the thought process of a Grandmaster to that of an expert (a much weaker, but quite competent chess player), you will often find that the Grandmaster consciously looks at less, not more. That said, the chunks of information that have been put together in his mind allow him to see much more with much less conscious thought. So he is looking at very little and seeing quite a lot."*
>
> – Josh Waitzkin – The Art of Learning

> *"Practice is funny that way. For days and days, you make out only the fragments of what to do. And then one day you've got the thing whole. Conscious learning becomes unconscious knowledge, and you cannot say precisely how."*
>
> – Atul Gawande, Surgeon

Such grandmasters and surgeons have successfully chunked their deep skills and knowledge upwards. By learning intricate and complex details of their craft so thoroughly at an unconscious level, they can now look at very little but see a huge amount.

TO-DO LIST

- [ ] **Ask "chunking up" questions to see the whole picture.**
- [ ] **Ask "chunking down" questions to understand the details.**
- [ ] **Consider how to apply some Van Gogh level chunking to your own life.**

DAY 13

Subliminal messages – do they work?

"It's the repetition of affirmations that leads to belief. And once that belief becomes a deep conviction, things begin to happen."

– Muhammad Ali

Affirmations are positive statements that allow our unconscious mind (Day 11) to begin to align with our conscious behavior. One of the first people to look into affirmations was an innovative 19th-century French psychologist named Émile Coué. He encouraged his patients to walk around and say out loud, "Day by day, in every way, I'm getting better and better." They were encouraged to do this up to 20 times a day. (Don't worry, we will be doing this in a less laborious way.)

Affirmations

Coué made some of the first discoveries around affirmations and how they can often work well in realigning the unconscious mind. He used a short statement that assumes the outcome is possible and achievable.

Set Your Own Affirmations

Make them positive, and what is happening now. Note: this is different from outcomes. Here's my affirmation on writing this book.

- *Every day I'm enjoying writing and getting closer and closer to finishing this book.*

Here's another.

> "My happy thoughts help create my healthy body,"
> – Louise Hay

If you don't fancy walking round muttering affirmations all day, then there is perhaps a simpler solution.

Automated affirmations

Subliminal messaging is controversial, but we can actually use it to help us with our NLP affirmations. It is a different and fun way to learn about them.

Psychologists have long agreed that flashing words too quickly for the conscious mind to register can have some limited effects in the lab (1). In 1957, the marketer James Vicary repeatedly flashed brief slogans during a movie. They said, "Drink Coca-Cola" and "Eat popcorn". These were subliminal messages that were too quick for the conscious mind to see and register. He claimed the sales of popcorn and Coca Cola increased by 18.1% and 57.7%. How sneaky, and how cunning to do this without people realizing.

The public responded with outrage. In 1962, Vicary admitted he didn't do enough research before going public – his study was a hoax. However, the idea of subliminal messaging had arrived. It eventually caused enough anxiety that it was banned in advertising.

But fast forward a few decades, computer programmers are now using this technology in a non-creepy way for the consumer – for us. The boffins have created programs that do all our affirmations for us. You can set these messages yourself. At various times during the day, these will flash on your screen for a split second and then be gone again. And the messages are so quick you don't even see them – unconsciously, you just start to notice changes being made. How sneaky, how cunning to do this without your mind realizing. It's not creepy anymore, and the message doesn't have to say "Eat Popcorn".

I'm running one right now on my computer (there are loads out there). As I work, I'm not really aware of the messages that are briefly flashing away every 30 seconds or so in the background.

The program works its unconscious mind magic without me having anything to do with it. It is on in the background as little or as often as you like. It has lots of pre-set messages to pick from, or you can add your own affirmations. I think one of the nice things about this is that, even by just opening the program and loading in the affirmations in the first place; you are changing the way you think.

But does subliminal messaging work? It seems like it might.

In one study, participants were found to be more likely to go off and buy a Lipton Ice drink if they were "subliminally primed" with the words Lipton Ice (2).

And this one's good. Murphy and Zajonc (1993) found that people had a better impression of random symbols if a computer subliminally showed a smiling face beforehand (3).

Affirmations can be a helpful way to relax and align the unconscious mind with conscious behavior. I'm always working to make sure these techniques are relevant in today's world for helping us understand and change our thought patterns and behaviors. Using them alongside technology is one way of doing that. As well as automated affirmations, you can try resetting your passwords with an affirmation or word that represents your affirmation (e.g. ExpertAtNLP30!).

TO-DO LIST

☐ Make affirmations positive, but not as if they've already happened.
☐ Use automated affirmations to align your unconscious mind with your conscious behavior.
☐ Try setting password affirmations.

DAY 14

Please Don't Read This

When I ask my three-year-old son to brush his teeth, he doesn't want to. However, mysteriously, when I ask him NOT to brush his teeth, he does. Why? There is a proven reason for this. Let's explore that today.

NLP And Language

Language can have a big impact on the way we communicate with ourselves and other people. In the introduction, I spoke about the power NLP linguistics had on my language when I was a radio presenter.

Today, we focus on just two of the many ways we can use language in NLP, by looking at "softeners" and "embedded commands".

Softeners

> - Make your language more persuasive by using softeners. We don't enjoy being ordered about, but these essentially soften an order. Good softeners to use are:

- I wonder
- Maybe
- Might
- Perhaps

Use these, especially in emails, where you can't convey tone. *I wonder if you might practice these techniques for the rest of the month?*

Task 2 – Embedded Commands and Negative Instruction

> Tell them what not to do

If I say: "Don't think about a yellow airplane," what do you immediately think about? The way the brain works, we have to process what a yellow airplane looks like before we can figure out the instruction to not to think about it. So you do indeed think of a yellow airplane. Fascinatingly, research shows such negative commands are often remembered even better than positive ones (1).

These negative commands and softeners both make use of an NLP principle called embedded commands, where you "embed" the command in a sentence in which you are telling them what not to do.

MY MIGRAINE HAS GONE

Dr. Milton Erickson (1901-1980) was a well-known hypnotherapist and a great inspiration to NLP. He used deliberately vague words to allow his clients to take the most appropriate meaning; the one which would help them get better.

Dr. Erickson's assistant regularly suffered from migraines. One day, he decided to try embedding commands and suggestions. While talking about day-to-day business, he used this language technique to focus on making her relax and feeling good. It worked. Her blinding headache went away, apparently within eight minutes (1) (2).

Here are some examples of how you could make these embedded commands and negative instruction work for you.

- "I don't want you to **feel better** just yet"
- "Please don't **practice this skill!**"
- "Don't **eat your broccoli**"

I wonder if you'll find these can help bypass any objection from the conscious mind and issue commands direct to the unconscious mind. My three-year-old hates being told what to do. Fair enough; so do I. But I bypass the objection from his conscious mind by using an embedded command with a negative instruction, because I believe it is a good thing that he cleans his teeth.

TO-DO LIST

- ☐ **Make your language more persuasive by using softeners.**
- ☐ **Combine embedded commands with negative instruction.**
- ☐ **Remember, these skills work. Always use your powers for good.**

DAY 15

Make Outrageous Ideas Succeed

> *"I'm not into all that Mickey Mouse nonsense."*
> – Tony Wrighton, shortly before he went to Disney World.

Yes, I was VERY skeptical of the "Disney dream". I like wholesome holidays climbing mountains, cold-water swimming and exploring nature. I like building fires and gazing at landscapes, not cheesy shows and rollercoasters.

Then I got asked to visit Walt Disney World for a whole week. For free. All expenses paid. Hmmm, perhaps I could swallow my principles and go anyway?

It was a trip to Florida in my capacity as a radio presenter in Manchester, UK. I was paid to work there presenting my show so, why not? Transported from the Manchester drizzle to the Florida heat, I loved the sunny optimism about the place. I ate well. I met lots of friendly people. I might have sung a few Lion King songs. I reached peak Disney when I rode the *Rock n' Roller Coaster* nine times in a row.

I was forced to re-examine my beliefs about Disney (the map was once again, not the territory). These days, I still love wholesome holidays up mountains, but I'm also (whisper it quietly), kind of looking forward to my son being old enough to ride *The Tower of Terror* with me.

Walt Disney himself used to say "If you can dream it, you can do it," and I could see the result of that thinking everywhere I went at Disney World. He made outrageous ideas succeed. In fact, the whole place is one big outrageous concept that just kind of works. Years later, I learnt about an NLP technique that helps us to think like Walt.

The Disney Strategy

It's thought we often discard brilliant, crazy ideas that could be incredible because "they won't work," before we give ourselves a chance to think how they could work. Perhaps we need to hold onto big dreams (like Walt) but balance them with reality (also like Walt)

> This is the first of two days of techniques originally created by Robert Dilts and adapted by me. Dilts was a long-time student of Bandler and Grinder. Having graduated in Behavioral Engineering, he turned his mind to the set of skills known as NLP, with stunning results.

The Disney Strategy

1. Dreamer stage. (This is the fun bit.) Spend some time dreaming up some crazy ideas for your life/work/business/leisure. Be creative. Anything goes. All ideas are good – discard nothing. Enjoy the process. Write them down.
2. Realist stage. (This is also a fun bit.) Spend some time working out how you could make all these ideas work.
3. Critic stage. (Actually, this is also fun.) Now look for flaws in your ideas, and what could go wrong. Be critical. What could misfire? What weaknesses are there in your plan? If there are weaknesses – either a) discard, or b) go back to

the Dreamer stage and dream up some solutions to those gaps in your strategy. No flaws? You are good to go.

The Disney Strategy in action

Walt Disney's initial plan was to build a perfect self-sustaining city that had everything people ever needed. 20,000 people would live there, traffic would be kept underground and the community would be carefully controlled. Disney World was only a small part of his original bigger project called EPCOT (Experimental Prototype Community of Tomorrow). Walt Disney's original plan was never realized because his board of directors considered it too ambitious. Instead, EPCOT was turned into a theme park. (1)

Disney's *Dreamer* ideas were big, wonderful grand ideas. Once they'd gone through the *Realist* and *Critic* stage they were still wonderful, and achievable too, as can be witnessed at today's Disney World theme parks all over the world.

So how can you use NLP to come up with some inspired ideas? Use the Disney Strategy and see what happens.

TO-DO LIST

- ☐ **Use the Disney Strategy on your outrageous ideas and dreams.**
- ☐ **Apply relentless realism and be critical. See the flaws, then dream up solutions.**
- ☐ **Hold onto big dreams (like Walt), but balance them with reality (also like Walt).**

DAY 16

Construct A Mind Pyramid

"Change is not a four letter word...but often your reaction to it is!"

– Jeffrey Gitomer

Making changes can be difficult. Adapting to new ways of thinking can be challenging. The "Mind Pyramid" can help.

It is adapted from the NLP technique called Logical Levels, (thanks again to Robert Dilts), with which we can assess what's going on at every level of our life. Explicitly stating what's going on at these different stages of the pyramid is one of the most important tools for behavior change we can use.

Here's an example. Claire has convinced herself she'll never be able to learn NLP. The skills are just too complicated. Even when she reads an easy-to-understand book like *Learn NLP*, she just can't quite grasp it.

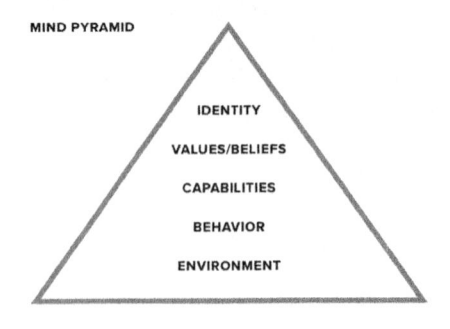

MIND PYRAMID

- IDENTITY
- VALUES/BELIEFS
- CAPABILITIES
- BEHAVIOR
- ENVIRONMENT

Logical Levels

Claire believes she can't learn NLP (behavior and capabilities). This sabotages her ability to become an NLP expert in 30 days. So she travels down the pyramid to ask questions about herself and NLP.

She arrives at 'beliefs' and asks herself what her beliefs are about NLP and her own ability. She discovers *she doesn't believe it is possible for her to become proficient at NLP.*

Ah. Suddenly we've found a potential answer. For Claire, the work needs to be done at a beliefs and even identity level (perhaps with hypnosis or other NLP tools), not at the level of behavior or environment. If she doesn't believe she can be great at NLP, she's not going to be.

> "The biggest barrier to positive change at any level—individual, team, society—is identity conflict. Good habits can make rational sense, but if they conflict with your identity, you will fail to put them into action."
>
> – James Clear, Atomic Habits

As well as at an identity level, perhaps Claire also needs to direct her gaze elsewhere on the pyramid. For example, on values, *does she actually believe it's important to learn NLP in the first place?*

Changes can appear anywhere in the pyramid. Now you try it.

- ➢ Think of an area where you feel a bit stuck or are struggling.
- ➢ Use the Mind Pyramid to work out where you need to change. Start at the top and work down.
- ➢ Examine your identity, values and beliefs, capabilities, behavior, and environment in this particular area.

> Which level provides the most useful information?

Here's an example. I have a problem. I snack on delicious white bread every time I see it in the bread bin.

- IDENTITY: My identity is that I like to be healthy, and that includes eating balanced meals and not snacking on delicious white bread.
- VALUES/BELIEFS: I believe healthy meals involve a balance of fats, carbs and protein. I don't believe it is healthy to snack on delicious white bread all day.
- CAPABILITIES: I am capable of going without delicious white bread, I'm just not very good with temptation when it's there.
- BEHAVIOR: I snack on delicious white bread every time I see it in the bread bin.
- ENVIRONMENT: There is lots of delicious white bread in my bread bin.

There's lots to work with here, but one glaringly obvious solution seems to be at the bottom of the pyramid, at the ENVIRONMENT level. If there wasn't white bread in the bread bin, I wouldn't be able to eat it. Therefore I should set up my environment to not have white bread in it.

Of course, this is a brief example and you might want to spend much longer at each level.

I used Logical Levels in the *30 Day Expert* title *Stop Scrolling* to help readers reflect on why they wanted healthier screen boundaries.

I gave the example of a friend of mine who has a young son. When her toddler was engaged in a game or wanted her attention, Anna often found herself on her phone, checking a message or idly scrolling. (As a parent of a young, boisterous boy, I empathize with Anna.)

> **OTHER APPLICATIONS OF THE MIND PYRAMID**
>
> You can use the Mind Pyramid when modeling others too. Start by learning from their behavior, environment and capabilities – the nuts and bolts of what they do. Who do they surround themselves with? What is their behavior? What are their capabilities?
>
> Then direct your attention to their values, beliefs, and identity. What do they believe is important about what they do? What are their values?
>
> What can you learn? Which level provides the most useful information? (SPOILER: People love to model behavior and environment, but in my experience the top levels provide rich answers that can be even more helpful.)

She examined herself at the values level and said,

"Those are not my values. That's not who I am. I've got to change that. I've got to put the phone down and put it away when I'm with my 18-month-old son."

It's easy to make changes at an environmental level (surroundings, people around you), behavior (what you can change), capabilities (how you can change). But gaining understanding at the top of the pyramid is sometimes more useful.

- If Anna remembers her strong value that it is important to be present with her son, it means her behavior is more likely to be that she switches off the tech distraction.
- If Claire believes she is someone who can successfully learn NLP, the changes she's made to her environment, behavior and capabilities are more likely to stick.

By studying yourself (or others) at every level of the pyramid, you can figure out at which level change is required.

TO-DO LIST

- ☐ Think of an area where you feel stuck or are struggling.
- ☐ Use Logical Levels to analyze every aspect and work out where you need to change.
- ☐ Which level provides the most useful information?

DAY 17

High Levels Of Focus And Deep Relaxation

> *"My mom hypnotized me and a wart came off my hand."*
> – Duncan Trussell, comedian

A hypnotic state is any altered state. But the H word gets a bad rap. Maybe that's because, when people think of hypnosis, they think of people prancing around on a stage pretending to be a chicken. However, it has lots more to offer than clucking.

Hypnosis can help us alter thought patterns, reach goals, calm nerves, increase focus, change habits and reduce anxiety. Popular neuroscientist Professor Andrew Huberman describes it as combining "high levels of focus and deep relaxation" (hence the title of today's mini-chapter). I use it almost every day – mostly the self-hypnosis format which you'll learn. It's a big part of NLP, and it has helped to create clear, positive changes in my life.

In case you're not fully convinced, let's quickly geek out on the research.

- Hypnosis has been found to be effective at treating pain, IBS, asthma and anxiety (1).
- Phobia patients who received hypnosis were over two and half times more likely to feel better than those who didn't (2).
- Hypnosis helps with insomnia, and extends restorative slow-wave sleep. Researchers found deep sleep in

participants who listened to a hypnosis tape at bedtime increased by 80% (3).

The studies go on and on, and you'd be surprised by how many people use it.

> Many famous people throughout history have used hypnosis. Here are three examples.
>
> - Albert Einstein reportedly came up with the theory of relativity during a self-hypnosis session.
> - Thomas Edison practiced hypnosis regularly and was a fan of "hypnagogic states" (the place between sleep and wakefulness).
> - Basketball star Michael Jordan practiced hypnosis and meditation before matches.

In some ways, everything you are learning throughout this program feeds into hypnosis. But it's worth dedicating some time to the power of hypnosis and how you can benefit from it.

Note: as already covered, we are not talking about manipulation here. We want you to use NLP and hypnosis to take control of your life and help other people do the same.

Hypnosis

Here are two "altered, hypnotic states" for you to try right now on yourself.

Self-hypnosis 1 – Parachute Hypnosis

"The mind is like a parachute. It works best when open."

– Frank Zappa

Let's open up our parachute mind with my adaptation of a famous hypnosis skill known as the Betty Erickson Technique. Betty Erickson was married to Dr Milton H. Erickson, who had an immense influence on the world of NLP. Her brilliant technique proves what a Neuro-Linguistic powerhouse she was in her own right, and I've adapted it here.

As you try this light self-hypnotic NLP technique, you float gently down into an altered state.

You do this by fully occupying the mind. It actually creates a state of concentration that is so full on it effectively relaxes the brain.

- Be still. Concentrate on three things you can see. Go slowly, focusing on each one.
- Now put your attention on three things you can hear. Again, take your time.
- You can now focus on three things you can feel or touch. For example, the feeling of your shoe on your foot, or the seat you are sitting on. Again, go slowly.
- Continue to focus methodically on three things you can see, hear and feel. Go for different things every time – these can be anything external and encompass anything that your senses tune into; people, items, objects, something in nature and so on.

Keep going for a full minute. Enjoy the chance to float into a minute of quiet time.

Keep your focus. Your parachute is well and truly open.

Self-hypnosis 2 – Hypnosis By Numbers

Again, this hypnotic exercise works by focusing the mind intensely on one activity.

- At a stressful moment, take deep breaths and count backwards from the number 100,000 for one minute. Like this: 100,000, 99,999, 99,999, 99,997. If you lose your place or get the numbers wrong, go back to 100,000 and start the full minute again.

The tougher you find this, the more likely it is that you need it. It is tricky to concentrate on the numbers and get it right. This is good — the change in where you are directing your attention is important.

Remember, hypnosis can bring about new responses, thoughts, attitudes, behaviors or feelings. This introductory overview of hypnosis is just the start. We will return to it throughout the rest of the program.

TO-DO LIST

- ☐ **Use hypnosis to bring about new responses, behaviors or feelings.**
- ☐ **Start with self-hypnosis. (It worked for Einstein.)**
- ☐ **Use "Parachute Hypnosis" and "Hypnosis By Numbers"**

DAY 18

Hypnotic Language Patterns

> *"Hypnosis is real, man. It really does work."*
> – Joe Rogan, podcaster and comedian

NLP began as a research project by Richard Bandler (someone I have studied with) at the University of California. He was interested in the therapeutic effects of a type of therapy focusing on present experiences rather than the past. As he listened to taped recordings of a chap called Fritz Perls, he noticed the "particular word and sentence structures" which helped Perls be good at what he does (1).

Between 1972 and 1974, Bandler started to collaborate with John Grinder, a linguistics lecturer at the time. They developed the Meta Model (they loved a 'model') for gathering information and uncovering thought processes. They published some brilliant books with trippy '70s covers including *Trance-formations* and *The Structure of Magic I and II* (2).

From the end of 1974 onwards, they got really excited about combining linguistics with hypnosis. They went down the rabbit-hole of hypnotic suggestion and behavior change.

> *"If you say to yourself; 'It's difficult to get up in the morning', 'It's hard to cease smoking', then you are already using hypnotic suggestions on yourself."*
> – Richard Bandler

They started to study the work of incredible therapists, including Virginia Satir and Dr. Milton H. Erickson. Erickson was a pro-level hypnotist and hypnotherapist, and had years earlier revolutionized modern therapy, The inventors of NLP were blown away by his work. They used their now-famous modeling technique (Day 9) to model Erickson's language patterns. This was the beginning of The Milton Model (3). It maps out the various rules of hypnosis.

Bandler and Grinder enrolled in courses with Erickson so they could model him, and turned out to be extremely good at it.

Bandler had excellent behavioral modeling skills: he had a remarkable capability to mimic other people's behavior and the way they spoke. He also had an extensive knowledge of the new contemporary systems of psychotherapy.

– Carl Buchheit, Ph.D. and Ellie Schamber, Ph.D., Transformational NLP: A New Psychology.

Having trained with Bandler, I can vouch for these brilliant mimicking skills, and they obviously came in very handy when doing deep modeling work on Erickson. So what exactly did they learn?

The Milton Model

The Milton Model shows how everyday language, like that which we use in regular conversations, can be hypnotic.. It is extensive and detailed, so we're going to take it one step at a time, and practice a few elements today.

> ➢ The Double Bind: "Do you want to read the rest of this chapter now or later?' (Gives me the illusion of choice.)
> ➢ Mind Reading: "I know you are eager to learn more about NLP and hypnosis." (How do you know?)

- Lost Performative: "NLP is awesome." (Says who?)
- Lack of Referential Index: "People say this book is awesome." (Which people? They are unreferenced.)
- Cause and Effect: If you read this book, you'll be great at NLP." (If A happens, then B happens.)

Now you have a go.

- Write down a Double Bind *now or later* that gives the illusion of choice:

_____

_____

- Write down a Mind Read. *I know you want to practice this one.*

_____

_____

- *Lost Performatives are great.* So have a go at one of them now.

_____

_____

- *It's often said that NLP is easier if you practice it.* So now try writing down something without a Referential Index.

_____

_____

> *If you keep going at NLP, you'll soon become an expert.*
> It's time to practice Cause and Effect.

_____

_____

Essentially, the Milton Model of hypnotic language is based on vague and often non-specific language containing deletions, distortions and generalizations. When you start to challenge these patterns, you use the Meta Model (I told you they loved a model.)

To round off the NLP history lesson, the popularity of these skills grew rapidly from the mid 1970s onwards and spread worldwide. More recently, famous hypnotist and author Paul McKenna is widely regarded as one of the world's foremost practitioners of NLP. Indeed, he used to own the world's largest NLP Training company. (I was lucky enough to train with Paul and it was outstanding.) Paul is also a big supporter of Emotional Field Therapy (EFT), otherwise known as "tapping."

NLP BOOKS

Many of the original books on NLP are highly recommended and have hallucinogenic 70s covers. Unfortunately, they are in high demand as they are now out of print. In fact, I bought my copy of another of their books, *Trance-formations,* for more money than I have ever spent on a book before.

These books are outstanding, but unless you are a true NLP geek you may want to start with something a little more readable as you start to become an expert in this world. Still interested? I just checked and the hardcover of *Trance-Formations* is currently available online for $249.97. Now that's dedication to NLP. Thankfully this book is a bargain by comparison!

Elsewhere, as we've already seen, bestselling author and famous Chicken Souper Jack Canfield is an NLPer.

> "NLP is a powerful system of thinking that can accelerate the achievement of your personal and professional goals."
>
> – Jack Canfield

And Tony Robbins has spent many years as probably the world's foremost personal development trainer. He doesn't call his methods NLP, but he originally trained with Richard Bandler and there are similarities in their approaches. His *Unleash The Power Within* signature event combines NLP-related techniques with physical challenges such as walking across hot coals.

TO-DO LIST

- ☐ Start to practice Milton Model hypnotic language patterns in conversation.
- ☐ Play around with techniques like Double Bind, Lost Performative and Mind Reads.
- ☐ Notice when other people use this language while talking to you.

DAY 19

Unwanted Thoughts Suck

> "I think too much. I think ahead, I think behind, I think sideways, I think it all. If it exists, I've thought of it!"
>
> – Unknown

Unwanted thoughts suck, especially when they cause you anxiety or distress. NLP has a way to deal with them though. Let's see if it works for you.

With today's technique, we replace negative emotions with more positive ones. It seems like a big promise, doesn't it? But that's what the Swish Technique does. It is a technique to change how you or somebody else feels and acts, and one of the most famous NLP skills.

Essentially, it replaces something in your brain that you don't want with something that you want.

> ➤ Today, find a willing participant to try the Swish Technique on. Explain you are just learning and you'd like to help them feel good. If you haven't got a willing client though, then no problem, you can use it on yourself.

How does it work? Your client (or you) is directing their brain towards *this, not that*. Sometimes an NLP analogy refers to "rewiring" the brain; you could say you are rewiring your response to negative emotions.

The Swish Technique

1. Identify a person's unwanted state (or your own). Perhaps they feel nervous around somebody, anxious at work or stressed when they think about their to-do list.
2. Decide on a different, more helpful state. How would they like to feel? Ask them to make an image of how that would look in their mind. Make the picture colorful. Make it vivid. Get them to put themselves in the picture (be associated). Ask them to turn up the volume and make it loud, crisp and vibrant.
3. Now ask them to see in their mind of how they look when they're feeling stressed/nervous/whatever they are working on. For some, this can be painful, so make the picture black and white like an old TV. Make any sounds faint.
4. As they look at this black and white image, ask them to place the colorful, swish state right in the corner of this stressed-out image. Make it tiny.
5. When they're ready, swish their positive state so that it grows enormous, and completely covers the old, unwanted picture. (Make a SWISH! noise).
6. The unwanted picture swishes away into the background. Now get them to associate with their huge swish state in front of them: brilliant colors, clear, glorious sounds, and wonderful feelings.
7. Now clear their mind. I tend to ask them what they had for breakfast as it forces them to focus on something different. (This bit is necessary.)
8. Go through steps 1) to 5) again. Swish a few times until your client struggles to see the unwanted image and until they find it difficult to feel the negative state. You can swish more quickly each time. This whole process might take between 10 to 30 minutes.

> **SWISH!!**
>
> Do you feel a bit silly getting animated and loudly saying "SWISH!" whenever you introduce the new picture/state? I hear you. For years I felt a bit sheepish doing this "SWISH!" with clients. But they always reacted well to it. Now I just get on with it and happily SWISH! The best way is to practice a lot and find a style that works for you.

This is a core NLP skill that practitioners like to use for everything, from overeating to procrastination. It can even help with learning. In one study, participants who learned English vocabulary using the Swish Technique performed better in a vocabulary test than those taught with a dictionary (1).

It is also sometimes used with smoking. Personally, I find it ambitious to hope that a highly addictive behavior and substance (nicotine) can be overridden with this technique – in these instances I would go more in-depth with a client. Some practitioners insist that it works, but I believe it is better suited to subtle changes in an emotional response like anxiety or stress, where it is very helpful.

TO-DO LIST

- ☐ **Unwanted thoughts and behaviors suck. Use the Swish Technique to deal with them.**
- ☐ **Create more helpful states in different areas of your life.**
- ☐ **Practice using the Swish Technique on others. Make a positive change in the world.**

DAY 20

Dealing With Phobias

Fear and anxiety can have a crippling effect on our lives. So now we are going to study a classic NLP tool which means learning to live with painful memories in a more functional way. We don't forget those memories, but we do reduce the power they have over us. This technique works for phobias and traumas too.

Fast-Phobia Cure

The Fast-Phobia Cure is a classic NLP skill. Research supports its effectiveness: 30 employees diagnosed with PTSD or partial PTSD took part in a study on "rewind treatment" (based on the Fast-Phobia Cure). 93% of people rated it as "extremely successful" or "successful". The other 7% thought it was "acceptable". No one rated the method poor.

And the kicker...

The fact that the treatment was quick, easy and painless was commented on by many and most said they would recommend the method to others (1).

So the research shows that the Fast-Phobia Cure works. It's a technique that I've certainly used effectively many times with people. It's all about dissociating your mind from negative past emotions – and it works.

> With NLP, we can learn to live with painful memories in a more manageable way

Traditionally, this tool is set in an imaginary cinema with a big screen and makes use of the Association/Dissociation concepts we learnt previously. The participant watches themselves watching the episode (the dissociation bit) and then floats into the cinema screen in the moment they feel safe and secure (the association bit).

I have slightly adapted it to make it more relevant to today. I've updated it to use an iPhone rather than a cinema screen for these reasons.

The Grayscale Movement

There is a small but growing movement of people combating screen addiction by turning their phone screens gray. It is one of the iPhone accessibility features that cuts all color out of the device screen, and it makes the display rather boring.

As I showed in *Stop Scrolling*, the science shows it cuts much of visual excitement out of your feed and makes scrolling less addictive. In fact it's been found that the grayscale phone setting reduces anxiety and problematic smartphone use (2). Importantly, participants in the study also reduced their overall screen time. It works because of dissociation, and I think this adds an extra layer into this technique.

Remember, we can't just "forget memories". But we can learn to live with them better.

- The iPhone screen is smaller therefore there can be even more dissociation when watching through the initial negative event.
- Mobile phones, smartphones and devices are such a ubiquitous part of life, it makes more sense to use that in the technique.

- iPhones have a setting called "grayscale" which makes the screen black and white. It can help us to dissociate from negative emotions.

The Updated Fast Phobia Cure

Start by practicing this technique on yourself. If you want, you can work through it with someone else.

Choose a negative event from your past that you'd like to worry about less. (When starting out, don't pick the huge, traumatic one. Practice first with one that has a milder emotional response.)

- Imagine looking through a dirty, narrow window at an iPhone with a black and white screen.
- When you feel relaxed, watch the event unfold on the screen with you in it. Then, pause it at a moment when you feel safe and relaxed.
- Next, imagine climbing into the paused moment on the iPhone (bear with me here - this is where the magic happens). Your surroundings are now full color. Rewind the scene in a few seconds and pause it at the beginning.
- Climb back through the window and repeat the process.
- Remember, you are watching the event in black and white on the iPhone, then climb through the window and rewinding it in color.
- Repeat a few times and notice how the event begins to lose its emotional impact.

Here's how important these skills are. A brain imaging study at the University of Colorado found that it's possible to "update our memories", inserting new details. It found that imagination may be a more powerful tool for updating those memories than scientists previously believed.

Imagine a barking dog, a furry spider or another perceived threat and your brain and body respond much like they would if you experienced the real thing. Imagine it repeatedly in a safe environment and soon your phobia – and your brain's response to it – subsides (3).

Using NLP, we can reduce anxiety and stress caused by worrying about the past and focus on the present in a more healthy way. This can help us to let go of unnecessary thoughts and "update those memories" to live with the past less painfully.

DEALING WITH OUR "DEEP STUFF"

My podcast *Zestology* has featured (not-very-humble brag) some of the biggest names in health, medicine, science and wellness worldwide, and speaking to many of these experts, one theme pops up again and again.

<u>We can't really change and move on until we deal with our deep stuff.</u>

It has been a learning curve on my podcast (and in my personal life) to realize that all the diet, sleep and health hacks in the world were no substitute for dealing with deep issues that were holding me back. Using NLP alongside other methods such as EFT and psychotherapy has helped me do this.

TO-DO LIST

- ☐ **Deal with your "deep stuff" by using this adaptation of an NLP classic.**
- ☐ **Notice how you can start to *dissociate* from painful memories.**
- ☐ **Remember, we don't want to "forget the past" but learn to live with it better.**

DAY 21

NLP and your notifications

> *"Have you ever been deep in conversation with someone when your phone dings? It's far too tempting to check it, and even if you don't, your attention is compromised."*
>
> – Amy Blaschka

There is an NLP concept called the *Pattern Interrupt*. It works by interrupting a pattern of behavior or thoughts. It redirects our attention in an instant. It can be a positive agent for behavior change, but can also be used against us.

The Pattern Interrupt

Notifications on our devices are pattern interrupts, because they interrupt our behavior, and ask us to switch context. They can shorten our attention span. They load us with extra information. They "can prompt task-irrelevant thoughts, or mind wandering, which has been shown to damage task performance" (1).

If our notification game on our devices isn't on point, we spend our entire day getting interrupted. So let's create pattern interrupts that use tech to help us navigate everyday life. This is an effective real-world application of NLP that helps us to become finely attuned to the pattern interrupts around us.

Remember, learning Neuro-Linguistic Programming concepts and skills is important for two reasons.

- To improve your own life and make the world better.
- To become aware of when these tools are being used against you and affecting you negatively.

Pattern interrupts That Don't Help

- Start to notice when pattern interrupts are important (ie, an important message from a colleague), and when they distract you (ie., your friend sends you a "This dog is livin' the dream" GIF while you are trying to work). The average attention span is now just 8.25 seconds, largely because of pattern interrupts like lock screen notifications, banners, sounds, alerts, badges, vibrations and so on.
- Switch off the pattern interrupts that don't serve you.

Pattern Interrupts That Do Help

- Use "pattern interrupt" reminders on your laptop/mobile to take a break and change your physiology. (These can be simple alarms or calendar notifications). They pop up = your pattern is interrupted.
- Use "pattern interrupt" apps like the Pomodoro App. These allow you to focus deeply for 25 minutes, then take a break, stretch and move into a different posture. The bell goes after 25 minutes = your pattern is interrupted positively. You rest, recover, then refocus.

Notifications are just one example of pattern interrupts. There are loads of others. They are everywhere and can be literally anything that *interrupts your pattern*.

Here's a positive pattern interrupt I set up. I'm way too good at aimlessly browsing through news sites when I should be working. So I use a website blocker called *StayFocusd* on my laptop. It bans me from mindlessly scrolling through sites like *BBC* or *The Guardian* when I should be working.

- My **pattern** is to mindlessly go to news websites when I should be writing this book.
- My **pattern is interrupted** when I am blocked from visiting it.

This is a positive pattern interrupt for me, as it allows me to task-batch deep work tasks together, and leave looking at news sites for later in the day.

> THE NETFLIX PATTERN INTERRUPT
>
> Netflix has an ever-more-sophisticated AI algorithm to collect data on what, when, where and how you watch shows. It allows them to personalize your homepage with shows that grab you, even though you weren't necessarily looking for them. It's another example of a pattern interrupt, designed to interrupt "the risk of the user abandoning" Netflix. Historic data suggests 80% of users find shows in this way on the streaming service, and only 20% through browsing shows or "most popular" charts (2).
>
> In my experience, this pattern interrupt is especially powerful because the moment you linger on a particular show, it plays the trailer (uninvited), and potentially interrupts you again.

I was interested to explore the topic of notification pattern interrupts further, so I interviewed the author of *Deep Work*, Cal Newport. He talks about the "hyperactive hive mind" and suggests establishing alternative ways to collaborate that don't involve unscheduled messages. These include generating weekly reports that don't require an immediate reply. NLP and Cal's work combine nicely and you can listen to *Zestology* episode #325 for my interview with Cal.

TO-DO LIST

- ☐ Notice everyday pattern interrupts and whether they are positive or not.
- ☐ Switch off pattern interrupts that don't serve you.
- ☐ Use positive pattern interrupts to create periods of rest and recovery through the day.

DAY 22

Decision-Making

> "I don't know about you guys, but when I have to make a decision I analyze the situation, evaluate the risk, take measures to limit the consequences and then I completely screw up."
>
> – Unknown

We've now completed three weeks of the *Learn NLP 30 Day Expert* program. And so from today onwards, we go out into real world scenarios applying our NLP, revisiting skills already mastered and learning some new ones too.

On Day 22, we look at decision-making.

Congruence

Authenticity is one key to making decisions. In NLP, we call it something slightly different – *congruence*. Congruence means your actions and your intentions align with your values and beliefs (so basically, authenticity).

It is something we should aspire to.

- Be congruent in your work and the people you deal with. That means being genuine and true to yourself and your values.

When you come from a place of authenticity, you can fulfill your potential and, importantly, enjoy the journey along the way.

> **AN EXAMPLE OF CONGRUENCE**
>
> To learn more on this topic, I approached one of my all-time favorite authors and podcasters. Chris Ryan PHD is a *New York Times* bestseller translated into more than 20 languages, but – as he told me – he doesn't have much money. So what gives?
>
> It all comes down to him being congruent with his life principles. He told me that somebody once said to him, *"Chris, there are two currencies that you'll spend throughout your life. One is money and the other is time. You can always get more money, but you'll never get more time."*
>
> Chris is in his 60s now. He's always followed this advice, doing what he wants and traveling where he wants. To him, life is about meaning, not possessions or riches. That's congruence. You can hear my interview with Chris on *Zestology* episode #244.

Now let's use congruence to help your decision-making, by combining congruence with Logical Levels (Day 16).

Logical Levels

Okay. You have a big decision, and you are not sure what to do? Great, use congruence with Logical Levels (Day 16) to help you make a decision that is most authentic to your personality.

- ➢ Take a big decision or dilemma. Perhaps it has something to do with a job, a contract, a client, a relationship, or a life opportunity. Then travel up the Logical Levels pyramid.

Ask yourself; what is your identity? What do you strongly believe in? What is important to you as a person? Do these things align with this decision? Would you be acting with congruence with a particular course of action?

When we ask ourselves what we really want, what we stand for and what we believe in, that helps to make us congruent and helps us make informed decisions.

I once applied Logical Levels to a big decision of my own. I had been offered a highly-paid job in journalism in an unusually quiet part of the world. If you've been to the North Kent coastline of the UK, you will know that it is exquisite but often sleepy. The job would be stimulating, mostly doing what I wanted to do, and it was where I wanted my career to go. The money was also good – so it was a tempting offer. But I worried I would get bored moving out of the city. I just couldn't decide what to do.

Enter Logical Levels. Would a move to the country line up with my values, beliefs and identity? I wanted to see if my personality aligned with this job at the higher levels of the pyramid.

I asked what I wanted from life. Was it to move to a sleepy village in Kent? When I answered the question honestly, I realized that I wanted to be around people, to live in a rich culture and to contribute to that culture. As beautiful as it was on the North Kent coastline, there seemed very little to do once I finished my day's work apart from a walk on the beach. I wouldn't be able to attend all the clubs and groups that I was a part of in London anymore, or see my friends and family. I would be too far away.

I had my answer. My <u>values</u> are to be part of a busy community and contribute to the surrounding culture. Being in the heart of the action is part of what I believe to be important for me (<u>beliefs</u>), and so Logical Levels told me this job was not the right option.

> *"Authenticity is about being true to who you are, even when everyone around you wants you to be someone else."*
>
> – Michael Jordan

I haven't regretted that decision, as it aligns with my identity. As a penniless and jobless journalist I did cry a bit until the next, more suitable opportunity came along, but it was 100% the correct decision.

You may find the answer to a dilemma comes to you quicker than you thought when you start applying your new-found NLP techniques to your decision.

TO-DO LIST

- ☐ **Take a big decision you can't make your mind up about.**
- ☐ **Use Logical Levels to help you with the process.**
- ☐ **Aim for congruence (where your actions, values and beliefs align)**

DAY 23

Let Me Tell You A Story

> "Good stories surprise us. They make us think and feel. They stick in our minds and help us remember ideas and concepts"
>
> – Joe Lazauskas and Shane Snow, The Storytelling Edge

When I first started learning Neuro-Linguistic Programming, I struggled to explain to my family and friends why it was so helpful and so important. I would tell them about the wondrous discoveries that I was making with my classmates; The Law of Requisite Variety, the Double Bind, The Map Is Not The Territory! Is it any surprise I was met with blank stares?

So I tried again. "But guys, you're going to love The Fast-Phobia Cure, The Swish Pattern, Presuppositions!" Again, the sound of wind rustling. And rightly, because NLP isn't about long, technical names or abstract theories. It's about getting results and communicating better day-to-day with ourselves and others.

So I took a different approach. I told them the story of how I was testing out the NLP tools on my radio show (see Introduction). I explained how my listening figures had climbed considerably since using these. I said how happy my boss was with me, and how my work was flourishing because of these strange new linguistic skills I was trying out.

Ah! Suddenly they were interested. "Really?" they exclaimed. "Tell us more, so we can learn this stuff too."

Storytelling

The story above is simply told to explain **the power of the story**.

Storytelling is a critical skill, important in almost every area of life, but it's often overlooked.

In NLP we sometimes refer to it as metaphor. When you tell people a story or use a metaphor, they relax. They want to know how it ends. As you tell your tale, you can weave in your point. It's a subtle, yet compelling way to get your point across.

> *"The most powerful person in the world is the storyteller."*
> – Steve Jobs

So use metaphors (real or imaginary). I told a story in this mini-chapter to make a point about the power of storytelling. I weaved in my point at the end. I'm not saying I told my story about learning NLP particularly well, but hopefully you get my point.

- ➤ How can you tell a story to make your point? Think of an area where you'd like to be persuasive. Now think about how you could fit your message to a story.

Rich, sensory language

Here's a key point about storytelling that will help a lot.

- ➤ When telling your stories, appeal to people's senses. Use rich sensory language and focus on the submodalities you learnt about on Day 4.

Example: Your colleagues are not taking their full allocation of holiday and they're exhausted. They've been doing a great job, but are working too hard and stressed. Why do they refuse to take time off? You want to encourage them to take a holiday.

- Option 1: You tell them; "you need to take a break, it's good for you."
- Option 2: You take a more evocative approach; You tell them how you appreciate their hard work, but they need to balance it with time out. You tell them about a recent holiday you had. You describe the rich hues of the blue you could see in the water, the feeling of the warm air gently enveloping you, and the sounds of the waves lapping gently like little kisses against the shoreline. (Okay that might be going a bit far.) Tell them how good it felt to unwind and relax in that delicious warmth, and maybe even describe some of the succulent dishes you ate. And remember to tell them that deep, warm feeling of calm you felt when you'd slept well for a week.

What is more persuasive? Option 1 or Option 2? You can make your point better with a story that appeals to the senses.

I'm currently watching a Western drama TV miniseries called *The English*. It's set in 1890s Oklahoma, and the setting is gorgeous. I feel like I'm there when I watch it. Every sense is amplified, the endless sunlit landscape of the old West, the gentle rustle of the wind, the hum of the flies. (Viewer advisory: the violence in it is also visceral, and brutal). Most brilliant film and TV dramas work because they powerfully connect to our senses, and that's why we want to use NLP in our storytelling.

Today's musings on storytelling were inspired by my experience on NLP Trainer Training. This was the final stage in the long process involved in becoming an NLP teacher, and mostly focused on NLP presentation skills (or "platform skills" as they called it).

It was mainly storytelling skills and I loved it. One idea that didn't resonate though, was that we students were encouraged to dress one notch smarter than our audience when teaching NLP. We were told, "it will give you authority".

I tried this many times. But I hated it. I don't enjoy wearing suits and overly smart clothes. Perhaps it's because I had to wear a suit and tie for years when presenting on TV. I'd rather wear something casual. It just feels more congruent.

Nowadays, if you come and see me do an NLP presentation, I'll be the scruffy one in a T-shirt.

TO-DO LIST

- ☐ Practice telling good stories. When you tell people a story, they relax.
- ☐ Appeal to people's senses to tap into their emotions.
- ☐ Tell your tale, hook them in, then weave in your point.

DAY 24

Mood Boosters

"Does the name Pavlov ring a bell?"

"No, but it makes my mouth water"

– NLP Dad joke.

We covered the famous Russian scientist Ivan Pavlov on Day 1. You'll remember he'd ring a bell as his dogs were being fed. After a while, he could ring the bell, and his dogs would salivate even when there was no food. A stimulus (in this case food, then the bell summoning the thought of food) could elicit an automatic response.

That's anchoring. It is such a core NLP skill that we return to it today and apply it to some real-world examples. We are going to play around with different types of anchors that you can bring into your own life.

Chaining Anchors

Start to think about the music that makes you feel good.

Music is a great way to use anchors effectively and simply to feel good (think Bill Withers' "Lovely Day", rather than Daniel Powter's "Bad Day"). It also is a perfect way to use an NLP anchoring skill called *chaining anchors*. This is where you gently move from one state to a different one using a chained series of anchors (songs).

> **SOME GOOD FEEDBACK**
>
> A common NLP kinesthetic anchor is to anchor a feeling to the touch of a thumb and forefinger. That's something I once taught a private group of mine; afterwards I had a lovely email from Karen in Sweden.
>
> *I am the Sales Director for a major beauty company. I am quite energetic and love to be on the go. And you can only imagine how lost I felt when I was badly hit by a virus a month ago. The doctor ordered me to take it easy to get rid of it or it might get worse. Yikes! I had an event coming up. I had no backup plan and I just HAD to do it. Every time I took any exercise my heart just sped up and I got dizzy, confused and exhausted. The doctor said it would disappear if I slowed down for a couple of weeks, but of course I still had to present this event.*
>
> *The day beforehand (guess what – it was Friday 13th too), I tried the anchoring you taught me. I'd used it before but not to slow down, just to pump me up. It was so great.*
>
> *Saturday, I held the event and I was teaching for 6 hours. Each time I felt the hammering start I manage to slow it down again via anchoring. Even on stage! So much easier than meditating for 20 minutes four times a day (one is more than enough to manage). Fascinating. Thank you so much again.*

It's difficult to go from feeling Radiohead to Wham in a few moments. That's where the process of "chaining" anchors comes in.

This means that you take your current emotional state, and slowly and carefully lead it by the hand into a more relaxed one. The best way to do this is with a playlist. Here's an example. Your friend wants to feel happier. So build a four-song playlist together.

- Ask them to pick a song that makes them feel neutral.
- Ask them to pick a song that makes them feel a bit happy.
- Ask them to pick a song that makes them feel very happy
- Ask them to pick a song that is literally their number one happy song of all time.

Think of it as like slowly ushering a friend by the arm onto their favorite sofa so they can feel a little bit better. That's chaining anchors, a technique I almost always use with playlists as it is something people enjoy and find effective.

Tech Anchoring

There is a way to instantly change your mood on Monday mornings (or any other time). And that's by using the video function on your iPhone, laptop or GoPro, whatever it is you've got.

Watching videos on your phone may not seem like the most sophisticated of techniques, but it is undoubtedly tapping into the power of anchoring. Scientists worked out a long time ago that our brains don't differentiate between real experience and imagined experience, creating that "Pavlovian response" (1). As a result, we can quickly and effectively take our minds to a more positive place on a Monday morning.

> This is ridiculously simple, but an exercise to get you to tune into how anchors are everywhere. Next time you're somewhere amazing – shoot some video. Just a minute's worth. And then watch it when you need to lift your mood. (I told you it was simple.)

I recently met someone who lives by the beach. Every morning he stands at his window and looks at the waves for five minutes, and nothing else. It sounds like an idyllic location, and he says that view sets him up for the day. The problem was, he found when he was away on business, he didn't have that view, so he didn't have his calming start to the day. So he took a video of the waves. And now he has his view wherever he is.

All of this is anchoring.

One of my favorite videos is of me on the beach with my wife and young son when he was a baby. There he is, gurgling in front of the camera as the waves lap gently in the background. It is a visual anchor that links me to how I felt at the time. Honestly, I love watching it. It makes me feel a little happier and relaxed when I look at it, so it is a powerful anchor for me.

TO-DO LIST

- [ ] **Try "chaining" emotional states together to gently change your mood.**
- [ ] **Build a "Chaining Anchors" Spotify playlist.**
- [ ] **Create "Pavlovian responses" by watching videos of amazing places or your kids goofing around.**

DAY 25

Improve Your Relationships

> *"Relationships can make you feel in bliss, and relationships can make you feel like you are in hell."*
>
> – Esther Perel on Zestology

When our closest relationships are firing, everything in our world seems to work better. Sure, we might take it for granted. But a wonderful and supportive partner enriches our lives in so many ways, and allows us to reach our full potential.

Conversely, relationship stress wears us down. It is the biggest energy sap you could think of; constant arguments, nagging or turmoil does not make for a cheerful person or happy couple. To improve my podcast listeners' relationships, (okay, and my own), I approached the foremost relationship expert in the world, Esther Perel. We met in Pasadena, California and spoke about the value of nurturing relationships.

She told me that one of the most important things is simply to be kind. See the good side of people. Think about the other person. Engage with them. Make the other person feel like they matter and their presence makes a difference.

After the interview, I sat in my hotel room thinking. It occurred to me that one brilliant way to apply Esther's wisdom is with the NLP concept known as "perceptual positions." I've tried to use it ever since in my own most important relationships.

Perceptual Positions

We already know that The Map Is Not The Territory (Day 7). Now we take a look at some other maps. By appreciating things from other people's viewpoints, you avoid getting stuck in one way of thinking about a problem. So pick a relationship which is important (and perhaps challenging). You are going to take three "positions" in the exercise.

1. Yourself
2. The other person
3. A detached observer

- Sit down. Shut your eyes. Take some time to appreciate the relationship and its challenges from your own perspective.
- Imagine yourself floating up out of your seat and over to another chair, where the other person is sitting. Float down and associate with them and how they feel. How do they feel about you? What do they believe? Allow some time for the answers to come.
- It's worth connecting with the positives from this other position if they are reluctant to appear. What is it they believe about themselves. What is it that they love and appreciate about you? Fully associate with that love.
- Float up again and over to a third chair in the middle. Float down into the detached observer position. Watch both yourself and the other person from there.
- What do you notice from each person's perspective? What do you notice about their interactions? What advice would you give each of them separately, and both together?
- Float up and back to your own seat. Associate with your own body. What is different about the relationship and the situation? How can you approach events differently in the future? What can you change by altering your perceptual position?

> **CHANGE YOUR LENS**
>
> This Perceptual Positions exercise is remarkably similar to what relationship expert Esther Perel told me when we met in California. She said;
>
> *"You change lens. It's literally putting a new lens on you, and now you are going to look for the things they do that are kind."*
>
> By changing the lens, or position, we can start to appreciate the other person anew.
>
> *"Instead of looking for everything the other person does wrong, you start to look for everything they do right. And you start to tell them."*

Perceptual positions are one way that you can use NLP in your relationships. Another, which we've already covered is representational systems. (Day 4) How does the other person experience the world? Is their "primary sense" seeing, hearing or feeling? I'm very visual, and my wife is very kinesthetic. That means we know we experience every aspect of the world in different ways and (most of the time!) amend our language appropriately.

TO-DO LIST

- [ ] **Apply Perceptual Positions to your most important relationships.**
- [ ] **"Change the lens" and notice how your perceptions alter.**
- [ ] **Notice how this helps you associate more with other people's "maps of the world".**

DAY 26

Winning At Life

> *"The victory can often go to the one who wants it less: the one who can take competition in his stride, with relaxed muscles and mind."*
>
> – Simon Barnes

For over 15 years, I've combined two careers as an author and a journalist, primarily covering sport. In my TV career I've been lucky enough to work for some of the world's top channels, and travel across the world presenting shows including live football, golf, darts and more. I've also worked on some of the world's most niche TV sports – so, er, there isn't anything I don't know about ten-pin bowling.

I love to analyze the mental game of these top level sports competitors close up. After a few years of watching, I found there were certain NLP concepts that help people to win at sport and life.

Affirmations

Most golf players are better on the range than on the first tee. That's because it matters less.

> ➤ Try to stop focusing on the score. Concentrate instead on each moment. Stay present. Use affirmations (Day 13) and tell yourself you only care about how well you play. Paradoxically, this is more likely to make you win.

Dissociation

If you tell yourself you can't win, alter the way your internal voice sounds.

- ➤ Dissociate (Day 5), and turn it into a cartoon character, for example. After all it sounds sillier when Bart Simpson says it. Alter the submodalities (also Day 5) by making it quieter and moving it further away.

Anchoring

- ➤ Listen to some music beforehand and make sure the lyrics make you feel good. Use anchoring to help (Day 1) Tip: Pharrell may work better than Radiohead. Chain anchors with a pre-match playlist for extra impact. (Day 24)

Non-Verbal Communication

Non-verbal communication is often more powerful than verbal. (Day 2) So look like a winner.

- ➤ Chest out, chin up. Head high and breathe deep. Yes you feel foolish. Yes you look ridiculous. But it works and you can turn your present state into your desired state.

Swish Technique

Think about what you want to happen.

- ➤ Imagine a clear, bright picture of how you will look when you win, then a small, darker image of how you feel now. Then swish (Day 19) the bright image on top of the dark one and repeat until the small one is harder to associate with. Now run it again with sounds and feelings.

> **Seeing, hearing and feeling the win**
>
> Many top athletes incorporate Neuro-Linguistic Programming type skills into their training, even if they don't call it NLP. Check out how American Olympic skier Emily Cook uses all the senses when she visualizes.
>
> *"Visualization, for me, doesn't take in all the senses. You have to smell it. You have to hear it. You have to feel it, everything... I would say into a [tape] recorder: 'I'm standing on the top of the hill. I can feel the wind on the back of my neck. I can hear the crowd,' kind of going through all those different senses and then actually going through what I wanted to do for the perfect jump."*

Most of us don't need a *Braveheart*-style-speech before we go out to play sports. We need to calm ourselves down. Start to change these five areas and you can get that wonderful, yet sometimes elusive state of "relaxed muscles and mind".

"You play like you practice and practice how you play."
– Marcus Luttrell

NBD Theory

Great athletes train all their lives for a few big moments. However, if they start to remind themselves of the enormity of the occasion in those moments, the pressure can become too much.

So here's a theory I've developed to help you do better in big life occasions, from elite sporting events to wedding speeches to first dates. It cherry-picks some of my favorite NLP tools including association (Day 5) and Logical Levels (Day 16).

I call it NBD Theory. What happens when you tell yourself it's just another day? What happens when you stop caring so much and stick to your usual routine? What happens when you take a pause, smile, and say to yourself, "It'll all be okay – it's just another day. NBD." It'll help take the edge off your anxiety. The best athletes stick to their regular routine before the biggest games. Their attitude is: "No Big Deal (NBD)".

> NBD Theory means you tell yourself it's just another day. You *do exactly what you normally do* in big life moments. Same breakfast, same preparation, same headspace, same environment and behavior as much as possible. Big tournament coming up? You tell yourself: NBD. Big meeting coming up? NBD. Big date coming up? NBD. It's just another day.

Often (but not always), when you deliberately take the emotion out of things you are worrying about, it might help you to focus on the process and just get on with it. It can feel artificial at first, but it works.

TO-DO LIST

☐ **Win at life by forgetting about winning. Concentrate instead on each moment.**
☐ **Use music for state change (tip: Pharrell may work better than Radiohead.)**
☐ **Use NBD Theory. No Big Deal – it's just another day.**

DAY 27

Anxiety Is Horrible

> "Anxiety's like a rocking chair. It gives you something to do, but it doesn't get you very far."
>
> – Jodi Picoult, author

I am definitely one of life's worriers. I know all about anxiety. And NLP has helped me deal with it. I sincerely hope that it can help you deal with it too, as today's title is true – anxiety is indeed horrible.

We focus first on our unhelpful inner critic, and then reduce stimulation and slow down with an unusual mindfulness technique.

Dissociation

Buddhists sometimes call our internal voice a "chattering monkey" that sits on your shoulder and jabbers unhelpfully.

We've already looked at submodalities (Day 5), and something that works for many people is changing the space or texture of their internal voice by dissociating from it (also Day 5.) It sounds weird, but I've worked with lots of people who've changed the qualities of their internal voice and felt less anxious after doing it.

They might make it sound high-pitched, more whiny, further away, quieter or make other textural changes which reduce its power.

1. Work out where your internal voice is.
2. Wherever it is, imagine moving it to a completely different place, and push it away from you.
3. Now make it more muffled, like you are listening to a conversation in another room behind a closed door.
4. Now make it quieter. Imagine turning down the volume to almost zero.

We could describe many NLP exercises as powerful mindfulness tools that can help with anxiety, and, by playing with submodalities, you can achieve a powerful inner calm with NLP.

> "Turn down the volume of your negative inner voice and create a nurturing inner voice to take its place. When you make a mistake, forgive yourself, learn from it, and move on instead of obsessing about it."
>
> – Beverly Engel, author

Instant State Change

Instant state change is something we've looked at repeatedly in this program (Days 1, 17 19, 24 and more), and we are going to revisit some of the principles we learnt on those days now.

Our danger response – known as the sympathetic nervous system – tends to be switched on far more than we need. We are all so jacked up and over-stimulated day-to-day, that we need something to calm us down.

That's me, for sure. I can be a little too "on alert" and my brain often perceives a situation as stressful or dangerous, even when it's not. Grappling with a broken printer in the office does not, it turns out, count as a life or death situation. So when fight or flight kicks in, I use this technique for focus, clarity and to feel more grounded in the moment.

It's called Stop, Look, Listen, Smell or SLLS for short. Hunters have used versions of this for centuries. In a stressful or dangerous situation, a person follows this four-part acronym for focus and clarity. What I find particularly interesting about this is that it is actually very similar to the Betty Erickson Hypnosis Technique (Day 17).

> ➤ Stop what you are doing. Look around. Listen to your surroundings. Smell your environment – my favorite part of this technique. The sense of smell is one we use less than most of the others. So by focusing on it, it really brings us into the moment.

Veteran Jeffry Harrison wrote about the transition from the military to civilian life, and how this technique from his previous career turned out to help him be more present. It is an effective form of mindfulness.

"One particular day, I was attempting to buckle down and knock out several hours of important, but monotonous work. It was crucial I completed it that day, but my mind was struggling to stay focused, and my attention bounced around from other people's conversations to my phone to anything but what I needed to do. Time for a SLLS break! After five minutes of stopping and refocusing with SLLS, I was able to sit down with resolve and accomplish my work."

Like Betty Erickson's hypnosis technique, this shows that you don't have to meditate to practice mindfulness. Done properly, this slows us down and gets us into a more mindful state.

TO-DO LIST

- ☐ Change submodalities when life gets stressful. (But grappling with a printer does not count as a life or death situation!)
- ☐ Try SLLS (Stop, Look, Listen, Smell) for mindfulness
- ☐ Revisit the many instant state change techniques that NLP offers.

DAY 28

Are You Crazy Enough To Believe You Can Change The World?

> "If I believe I cannot do something, it makes me incapable of doing it."
>
> — Mahatma Gandhi

NLP has a concept known as *limiting beliefs*. These are decisions or beliefs we have made about our lives that limit us or hold us back. The thing is, these limiting beliefs are not necessarily true. Remember, The Map Is Not The Territory (Day 7)?

A lot of our limiting beliefs become embedded in childhood. Studies have found that our attitudes and beliefs come from the (often forgotten) past (1). It's worth asking if these are simply stories we've attached meaning to. NLP shows us that those stories can be changed, because they're just stories. And you can help other people/clients/friends/family do the same thing. Look out for their limiting beliefs too and help them change.

> "The people who are crazy enough to believe they can change the world are the ones who do."
>
> — Steve Jobs

If you want to make a difference, you have to actually believe you can.

Limiting Beliefs

(Do this with yourself or someone else)

- Think about something you would like to achieve which you haven't yet.
- Examine your beliefs around this issue.
- Identify any limiting beliefs - anything holding you back.
- Change the story with some of the powerful NLP tools you've learnt. Use a reframe (Day 9), affirmations (Day 13) or alter your inner voice (Day 27)

"Decide what you want, believe you can have it, believe you deserve it and believe it's possible for you."

– Jack Canfield

My example:

Here's my personal example of limiting beliefs. I want to become a talented chess player, and beat my friend John. It is achievable, as he's good, but not grandmaster good. In fact, I almost beat him once.

Here is how I used the limiting beliefs exercise to change the story.

Limiting belief: The thing is, I've known John for a long time. He was top of the class at math at school, and I was one of the most mathematically challenged. I've always told myself that.

Changing the story 1: I'm actually quite good at math, but didn't concentrate in math lessons at school.

Changing the story 2: Chess isn't really about math anyway, but about logic, strategy, art, creativity, and psychology.

LIMITING BELIEFS AND HIGH ACHIEVING

Success, of course, can be measured in many different ways, but there are long lists of prominent achievers who don't seem to have many limiting beliefs despite a non-conventional background.

- Oscar-winning actress Halle Berry. (She lived in poverty and stayed in a homeless shelter early in her career. In adversity she still managed to stay focused on her dream.)
- Entrepreneur Richard Branson. (He left school at 16 to start businesses, work hard, make money and have fun along the way.)
- Whole Foods founder John Mackey. (He dropped out of university and instead worked hard to learn the organic food trade from the bottom up)

For a long time, I carried with me a limiting belief that I'm bad at math, but I have now changed the story and reframed that belief.

What's my story now? I just didn't flourish in the learning environment at my school. I actually love learning. Discipline in learning is something I excel at. (I've made an affirmation to remind myself of this). Also, chess is not all about math, so I can beat John by being better at other skills.

TO-DO LIST

- ☐ **Become aware of your "limiting beliefs" and how they hold you back.**
- ☐ **Change your story to change your results.**
- ☐ **Revisit *reframing*, *affirmations* and *inner voice* skills for limiting beliefs.**

DAY 29

The Zeigarnik Effect

Have you ever crammed for an exam only to forget the information afterwards? Or been given a phone number and forgotten it the moment you put it in your mobile? This is the Zeigarnik Effect.

In 1927, a Lithuanian-Soviet psychologist called Bluma Zeigarnik found that waiters remembered orders only as long as the order was in the process of being served. Once the order was delivered, they couldn't remember it anymore. She observed that people tend to remember unfinished or incomplete tasks more easily than completed tasks, and so The Zeigarnik Effect was born (1).

As we are almost at the end of your *30 Day Expert* program, let's have some fun with the Zeigarnik Effect and NLP. I'll start with a concept that I learnt long ago; I would (not-very-modestly) say it made me a more effective TV and radio presenter. But how?

Nested Loops

The *Nested Loop* technique is an effective NLP storytelling and presentation device. Think of a loop as an open, unfinished plotline that keeps us on tenterhooks. This tool is for anyone who wants to be more interesting, compelling and persuasive.

The theory goes that the more loops (or plotlines) you open when telling stories, the more whoever is listening to you will a) be itching to find out what happens, b) be hypnotically lulled into not questioning the content of what you are talking about. Their critical conscious thought processes get bypassed.

> You'll find comedians, especially, use these open plotlines a lot (though they may not call them "nested loops"). They'll start a story, and return to it later in their set.
>
> Watch any comedy special on Netflix and see how many loops comedians open, continually returning to their open plotlines.
>
> Zeigarnik tells us it only makes the audience more interested to find out what happens, and NLP tells us these nested loops are a powerfully hypnotic way to communicate.

You open up lots of plots in one chat. The upshot is a powerfully hypnotic storytelling effect, as the conscious mind gives up following and simply sits back to enjoy the ride.

That's the idea, anyway. The more plotlines you open, the less their conscious mind analyzes what you are doing or communicating, and simply relaxes into it.

> ➢ Start a story (or loop), but don't finish it. Before you get to the punchline, start another story and another – as many as you want. Then close the "loops" in reverse order.

I told you how, a long time ago, I'd learnt an NLP training technique that completely changed the way I presented on TV and radio. That was a nested loop. The more I learned to open topics, and then circle back to them, the more I found I could keep people interested for longer. (And now I've closed that particular loop in this book.)

I use this technique in live presentations now. If you'd like to see this in action, head over to my site. There's a talk there I give away for free called *Supercharging Your Health With Biohacking,*

Mindset and NLP. It's part of the Starter Library on my site. Count how many loops I open and then eventually close.

NLP and Motivation

Zeigarnik taught us about more than just nested loops. I think her law also had something to say on motivation.

I write daily. When I sit down, I NEVER want to get started. I can find a million things to do that are seemingly more important. But I know now, after years of painful experience, that the best way to get over this procrastination is to click a timer which shows I'm now "writing for two hours". As soon as the timer goes on, I'm forced to at least think about what to write. It's an uncomfortable feeling. But five minutes later, I'm fully immersed.

The Zeigarnik Effect tells us we remember incomplete tasks better, and I believe we can apply this to motivation.

> ➢ Motivation doesn't lead to action, but action leads to motivation. The Zeigarnik Effect tells us the key is to just get started. Then we will be more motivated to get it finished, as it is an incomplete task.

"I never want projects to be finished; I have always believed in unfinished work. I got that from Schubert, you know, the 'Unfinished Symphony'."

– *Yoko Ono*

At the end of the day, I completely clear my to-do list. Our favorite early-20th-century psychologist suggests that, if I don't, I will take my work home with me and worry about all the unfinished items. So I clear the list, move any outstanding items to a 'future list', then switch off and unwind.

TO-DO LIST

- ☐ **Remember: we remember incomplete tasks better.**
- ☐ **We can apply this to storytelling – use NLP's Nested Loops techniques.**
- ☐ **Practice opening multiple "plotlines". It makes your audience more interested.**

DAY 30

And The Winner Is…

Emotional Intelligence is our ability to communicate with empathy and rapport. It is sometimes referred to as EQ, and perhaps just as important as IQ, but in a very different way.

> *"If you approach and engage with people with respect and empathy, the seemingly impossible can become real."*
>
> – Bob Iger

Daniel Goleman, in his book *Emotional Intelligence,* described EQ as the ingredient that separates star performers from the mediocre, and argued that anyone can gain these skills.

> OUR SUCCESS DEPENDS ON OUR EQ
>
> Research shows our IQ only accounts for 20% of our success at work, and in life, whereas 80% depends on our EQ.
>
> *While our intellect helps us to resolve problems, to make calculations or to process information, EQ allows us to be more creative and use our emotions to resolve our problems.* (1)
>
> Moreover, in a survey, 71% of employers said they value EQ over IQ (2).

I like to describe Emotional Intelligence as "street smarts" and my desire to improve my own emotional self-regulation and awareness was the reason I started learning Neuro-Linguistic Programming in the first place.

Happily, a recent study found a whole host of different NLP tools improve our Emotional Intelligence (3). This is why the combination of EQ and NLP is such an apt topic for our final day. In 2019, Kamarul Zaman bin Ahmad's research found five big emotional intelligence wins from using NLP. We've actually studied all five over the last 30 days, and today we'll revisit each tool, plus unveil the technique that did best of all in the research.

Here's what the 2019 study in discovered;

- The NLP skill of goal-setting (Day 3) can improve your self-awareness.
- NLP dissociative tools (Days 5, 26, 27) can improve the self-regulation dimension of emotional intelligence.
- NLP association (Days 5, 20) can improve self-motivation.
- NLP mirroring (Day 2) can improve your empathy
- Other NLP rapport skills (Days 2, 4, 23) can improve the social skills dimension of emotional intelligence.

In all cases, the NLP tools boosted mean scores by a significant amount. But one outperformed the others.

Is This The Most Useful NLP Technique?

The most successful technique in this particular research was the "dissociative technique" that we learnt on Day 5. Respondents were asked to remember an event that they still felt stressed about. Then, the researcher taught them dissociation.

Participants were asked to see the event through the third person view, and then change the "submodalities" of the mental picture by changing it from color to black and white, reducing the clarity and size and gradually pushing the picture further away. In other words, they were told to do exactly what we did when we learned about dissociation.

This one simple NLP technique improved scores in the study group by over 60%, and is a powerful one for you to return to in the future as you take your NLP expertise out into the world.

All that remains is for me to say congratulations on finishing the program. Well done. As a parting shot, here's a reminder that the set of skills you've been learning over the last 30 days can supercharge your life in every area. But you have to keep practicing. Don't let this book gather dust on your shelf (or your eBook shelf). It's all about using these skills and learning which ones suit you on a day-to-day basis.

Whether you are using association, dissociation, goal-setting, values, matching, mirroring, or any number of other techniques we've looked at, you can create positive change in your career, relationships, wealth, health and life by using NLP long into the future.

TO-DO LIST

- ☐ **Use NLP to help improve your emotional intelligence (EQ).**
- ☐ **Work on "self-regulation, self-awareness, and empathy" with NLP.**
- ☐ **Congratulate yourself. Completing this *30 Day Expert* program takes commitment and resilience.**

If you enjoyed this, please do review this book, it makes a huge difference. You can join the mailing list over at tonywrighton.com and get regular NLP updates. And now, a sneak preview of another *30 Day Expert* program you might like…

STOP SCROLLING

Stop Scrolling: Healthy Screen Time in 30 Days (Without Throwing Your Phone Away)

> *"Man who invented the mobile phone says people need to 'get a life'."*
>
> – Metro Newspaper Headline, 30th June 2022.

This book is for you if:

- You wake up and scroll before breakfast.
- You take your phone to the toilet (yes, you).
- You tap your dead phone for alerts.
- You feel on edge when you can't check your messages.
- You feel stressed, anxious, and busy, or you have a backlog of 18 messages waiting for a reply.
- You want to get more focused, creative, productive and happy.
- You are currently scrolling on your device for the 194th time today.

The science around scrolling is piling up. Too much screen time is bad for our physical and mental health. It is linked to an alarming cocktail of anxiety, depression, and poor diet, health and sleep (1, 2, 3). We now spend an average of almost six hours a day (yes, six) on email (4). Young US TikTok users average 87 minutes a day on that site alone (5). We are literally scrolling away our lives.

So over the next 30 days, you'll learn to

1. **Scroll a bit less.**
2. **Scroll a bit smarter.**

Each day is a mini-chapter containing a proven screen time change you can use straight away. And don't worry; you don't have to throw your phone away. We're just going to scroll a bit smarter, using NLP techniques and the latest in behavioral science. It's really pretty painless.

We're going to change our unhealthy screen habits, starting now. In the words of the man who invented the mobile phone, it's time to "get a life".

Hi, I'm Tony, and I'm addicted to scrolling. Or at least I was. I'm getting over it now, with the help of the techniques in this book. Here's a little more about me.

- I'm a journalist and wellness author. My books have been translated into 12 languages.
- I started writing about wellness and personal development two decades ago. Yes, pre-Facebook.
- I work hard at healthy online behavior. Yet I am still addicted to the tiny pleasures of a tweet, ping or like.
- Fun fact: pre-scroll addiction, my friend and I actually shared an email address when we went traveling in Asia. Yes, that's how innocent life was.

I've always had issues with focus and attention span. My science teacher once said in a school report that I was "bone idle". I may have been mischievous, but this was unfair. I love learning and working; I'm just easily distracted. I have to work really hard at focusing (so scrolling is my kryptonite).

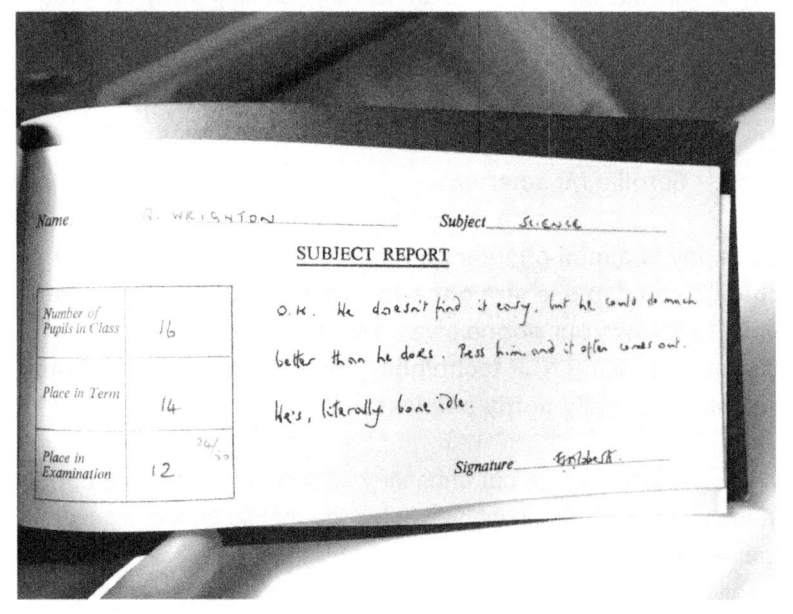

"He's, literally bone idle." *A very unfair school report. Perhaps my teacher should have focused more on his own poor grammar.*

This problem of distraction now seems to be affecting everyone, even people who didn't come near the bottom of the class at school because they couldn't focus. And it's because of screens. The number of hours per week we spend pixel-gazing is off the charts, but we just can't stop.

Over the course of this program, I will lay out some of the incredible science that shows just how distracting our screen time has become. And then we will reduce those distractions. We will stop, press pause and recharge.

This problem of distraction is not a new one

Frédéric Chopin was one of the world's most celebrated composers. He lived in Paris in the 19th century, and was an urban creature. He enjoyed living in the city and all of the distractions that life there had to offer. Obviously, this was 200 years ago and those distractions did not include a regularly refreshed TikTok feed. But there was still plenty for Chopin to amuse himself with in Paris.

Every summer he would escape the city and go to his partner's house in the country. Novelist Aurore Dupin (known by her pen name George Sand) had a retreat in the French countryside. Chopin found the pace of rural life painfully slow, but this was where his creativity became supercharged. The quieter pace meant fewer distractions, and he would write music more productively than he could ever do in the city.

Sand described the way that Chopin would wake early, have a simple breakfast and then spend the entire day composing, because *there was nothing else to do*. He would absorb himself for, as she described it, weeks at a time, on a single page of musical note-taking. After six weeks, he would often abandon all of his scribblings and go back to the original composition, which had been just right.

The more Chopin eliminated his day-to-day diversions, the more he was able to create his finest work. Truthfully, it wasn't all idyllic. Apparently he would sometimes sulk in his room and break his pens in frustration. Yet, this was all part of the creative process. His genius could only truly express itself without distraction and interruption.

Let's be honest, he was lucky he didn't have Instagram. Or a phone. Or a laptop. Or unlimited wifi. And despite having none of that, he *still* needed to escape the city to get his work done. This suggests this problem of distraction is not a new one.

Fast forward to today though, and all of our brains are overworked. Screens are now taking information overload to a level significantly more problematic than in Chopin's day. His sort of single-minded creativity and brilliance is becoming a rarity. Chopin was a world-renowned musician, and, to be at his best, he had to reduce the amount of information coming in. As Nicholas Carr observes in his excellent book *The Shallows: What the Internet is Doing to Our Brains:*

"When our brain is overtaxed, we find distractions more distracting."

We will explore this idea of *distracting distractions* in depth over the next 30 days. We will reduce our reliance on screens, and indulge in some healthy scrolling. And it won't involve locking yourself in your room and breaking your pens. You will feel happier, healthier, more motivated and more inspired, and you'll have a lot more time on your hands too.

REFERENCES

Day 1

1. https://www.simplypsychology.org/pavlov.html
2. https://www.science.org/doi/abs/10.1126/science.1195701

Day 2

1. https://www.researchgate.net/publication/251630934_Retail_salespeople's_mimicry_of_customers_Effects_on_consumer_behavior
2. https://www.researchgate.net/publication/233010541_Mimicry_and_seduction_An_evaluation_in_a_courtship_context
3. https://hbr.org/2020/12/want-to-win-someone-over-talk-like-they-do
4. https://www.sciencedirect.com/science/article/abs/pii/S174438810500071X?via%3Dihub
5. http://www.gremler.net/personal/research/2008_Rapport_CIT_JR.pdf

Day 3

1. https://psycnet.apa.org/record/1981-27276-001
2. https://www.researchgate.net/publication/336004061_The_Effectiveness_of_Neuro-Linguistic_Programming_NLP_on_Shooters'_Mental_Skills_and_Shooting_Performance

Day 4

1. https://www.sciencedirect.com/science/article/pii/S1877042814008428?via%3Dihub

Day 5

1. http://ellenlanger.com/books/counterclockwise/
2. https://pubmed.ncbi.nlm.nih.gov/20483844/
3. https://cyberleninka.org/article/n/336498

Day 6

1. https://www.bl.uk/collection-items/leonardo-da-vinci-notebook

Day 7

1. https://abcnews.go.com/blogs/headlines/2012/03/gps-tracking-disaster-japanese-tourists-drive-straight-into-the-pacific

Day 8

1. https://hubermanlab.com/the-science-of-vision-eye-health-and-seeing-better/
2. https://nlppod.com/research-support-for-nlp-eye-accessing-cues/
3. https://www.tandfonline.com/doi/full/10.1080/135765 0X.2019.1646755

Day 9

1. https://www.baumanrarebooks.com/rare-books/frankl-viktor/from-death-camp-to-existentialism/118063.aspx
2. https://www.psychologytoday.com/us/blog/stronger-the-broken-places/201712/reframing

Day 10

1. https://meaningring.com/2019/09/17/life-advice-from-rick-rubin/

Day 12

1. https://www.psychologytoday.com/intl/articles/199905/the-stirring-sound-stress
2. https://psycnet.apa.org/doiLanding?doi=10.1037%2Fh0043158
3. https://www.simplypsychology.org/unconscious-mind.html

Day 13

1. https://www.bbc.co.uk/news/magazine-30878843
2. https://www.sciencedirect.com/science/article/abs/pii/S0022103105001496?via%3Dihub
3. https://doi.org/10.1037/0022-3514.64.5.723

Day 14

1. https://psycnet.apa.org/record/2014-00787-008
2. https://www.academia.edu/10012114/Patterns_of_the_Hypnotic_Techniques_of_Milton_H_Erickson
3. https://www.nlpcourses.com/planting-ideas-peoples-minds/

Day 15

1. https://sites.google.com/site/theoriginalepcot

Day 17

1. https://www.ukhypnosis.com/hypnosis-research-evidence/
2. https://pubmed.ncbi.nlm.nih.gov/25928602/

3. https://www.sciencedaily.com/releases/2014/06/140602101207.htm

Day 18

1. https://nlpea.com/international-nlp-association-of-excellence-nlpea/history-nlp
2. https://www.landsiedel.com/en/nlp/history-of-nlp.html#introduction
3. https://hypnosistrainingacademy.com/milton-model-hypnotic-language-patterns-trance/

Day 19

1. https://www.semanticscholar.org/paper/The-Impact-of-Neuro-Linguistic-Programming-(NLP)-on-AfsaneMoharamkhani/49e9502b4b86c75273102c2d88b212f9a35d42b4

Day 20

1. https://www.hgi.org.uk/resources/delve-our-extensive-library/anxiety-ptsd-and-trauma/fast-cure-phobia-and-trauma-evidence
2. https://link.springer.com/article/10.1007/s12144-021-02020-y
3. https://www.sciencedaily.com/releases/2018/12/181210144943.htm

Day 21

1. https://dl.acm.org/doi/10.1145/2843948

Day 24

1. https://www.simplypsychology.org/pavlov.html

Day 28

1. https://www.researchgate.net/publication/254081446_Sources_of_Implicit_Attitudes

Day 29

1. https://www.simplypsychology.org/zeigarnik-effect.html
2. https://codeblab.com/wp-content/uploads/2009/12/On-Finished-and-Unfinished-Tasks.pdf

Day 30

1. https://www.sciencedirect.com/science/article/pii/S1877042812021477
2. https://press.careerbuilder.com/2011-08-18-Seventy-One-Percent-of-Employers-Say-They-Value-Emotional-Intelligence-Over-IQ-According-to-CareerBuilder-Survey
3. https://www.researchgate.net/publication/333834737_Examining_the_Effectiveness_of_Neuro-Linguistic_Programming_NLP_techniques_in_improving_Emotional_Intelligence_EI_scores

Printed in Great Britain
by Amazon